WJEC GCSE Poetry Collection

Sarah Basham
Caroline Bentley-Davies
David Grant
Consultant:
Stuart Sage

www.pearsonschoolsandfecolleges.co.uk
✓ Free online support
✓ Useful weblinks
✓ 24 hour online ordering

0845 630 22 22

Part of Pearson

Contents

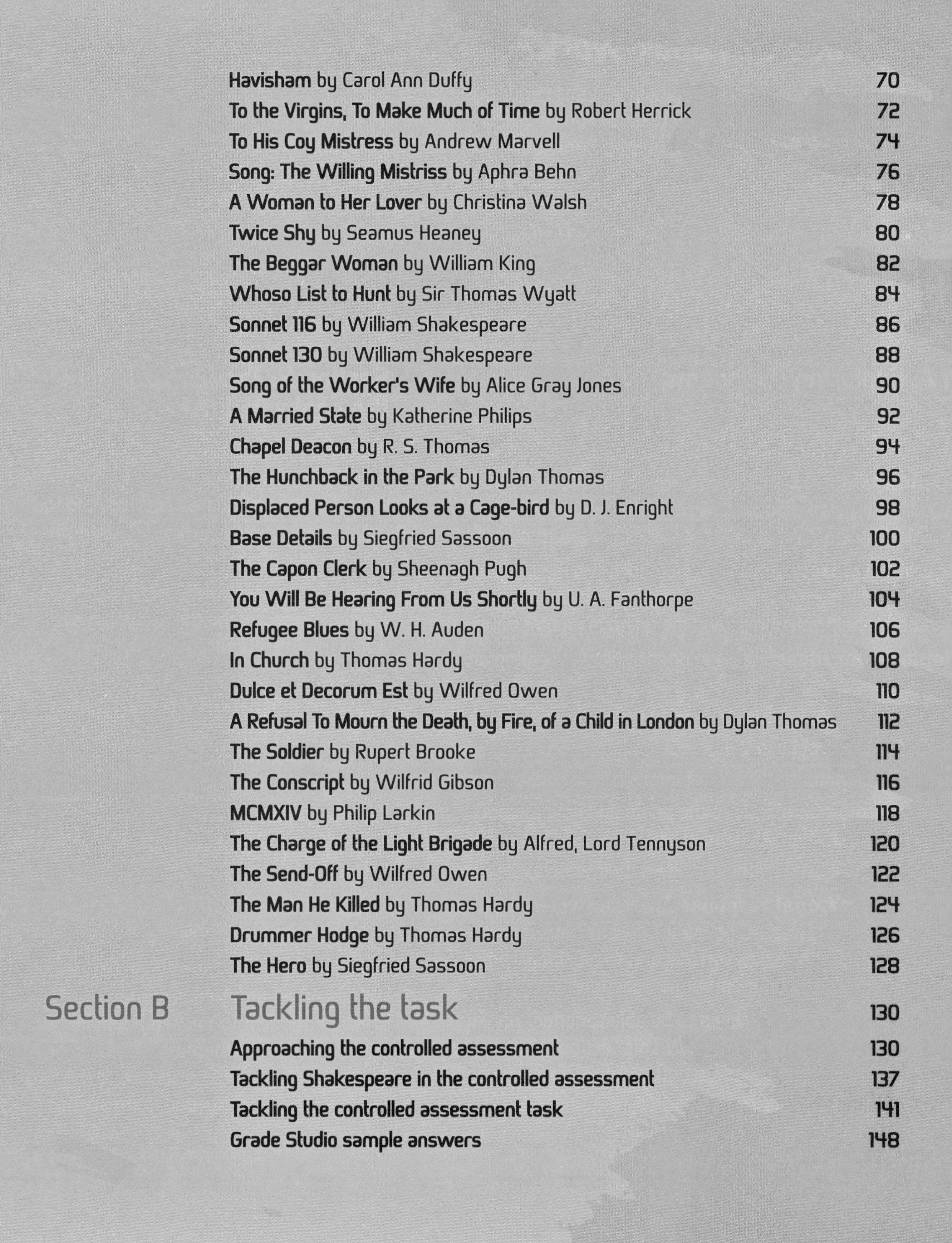

Introduction

How does this book work?

This book has been designed to help you raise your achievement in the WJEC GCSE English Literature (Unit 3) Poetry and drama (literary heritage) or WJEC GCSE English (Unit 3) literary heritage poetry and Shakespeare.

Your teacher will decide which GCSE is most suitable for you, but you will need to complete this task whether you are studying GCSE English or GCSE English Literature, and whether you are entered for the Higher or Foundation tier.

How is the book structured?

This book is divided into two sections.

Section A: Exploring the poems

This section looks at all the poems in the WJEC Poetry Collection. For each poem you will work through the following stages:

1 **First thoughts** After reading the poem for the first time you will think about your initial reactions. What is the poem about? How does it make you feel? What questions does the poem raise?

2 **Looking more closely** You will begin to focus on the language of the poem. You will need to annotate it, highlighting key areas and making notes to help you understand the poem in greater depth.

3 **Developing your ideas** For each poem you will develop an understanding of:
- theme (the ideas at the heart of the poem)
- content (what happens in the poem)
- viewpoint (the point of view or opinions of the speaker / poet)
- mood (the atmosphere/tone of the poem and how the poet wants you to feel when you read it)
- style (techniques used by the poet, and their effects).

4 **Developing a personal response** Analysing writers' language and techniques is very important, but it is just as important to consider how the poem makes you feel and to be able to write about your thoughts and your emotional reactions.

5 **Peer/self-assessment** You need to be able to reflect on your own work and know how to improve it. This section will help you look at your writing, consider its strengths and weaknesses, and re-draft it to improve and progress towards your target grade.

Section B: Tackling the task – the controlled assessment

This section focuses on preparing for the controlled assessment task. You will be shown how you will be assessed, and the assessment objectives that are used to decide your grade.

Your teacher will provide a task based on a theme. These are the themes you may be asked to write about:
- Love
- Family and parent/child relationships
- Youth and age
- Power and ambition
- Male/female relationships and the role of women
- Hypocrisy and prejudice
- Conflict
- Grief

The task will require you to:

1 write about your chosen Shakespeare play in relation to this theme
2 write about your chosen poem in relation to this theme
3 give your personal response to the two texts, making links and comparisons between them.

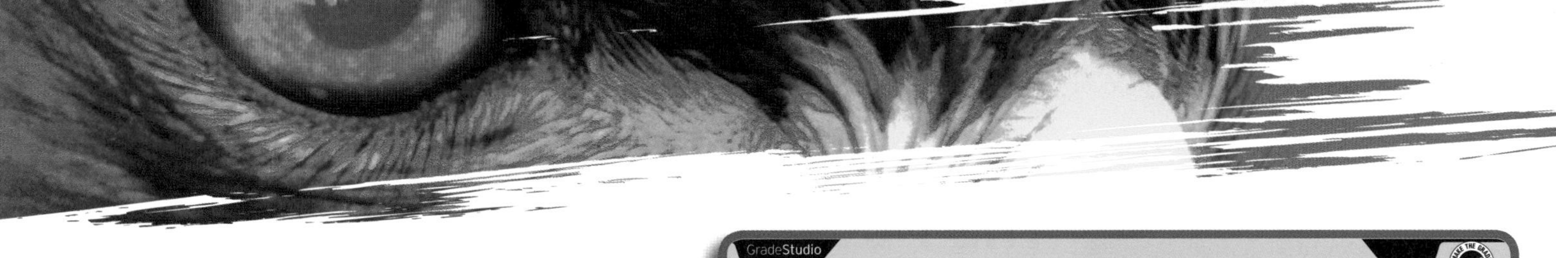

Section B also provides extracts from sample student answers with comments from experienced WJEC examiners. You will be able to see examples of all grades and identify the key features of each, which will help you to improve your own writing.

Together, the two sections of this book will enable you to write confidently and help you to achieve your best.

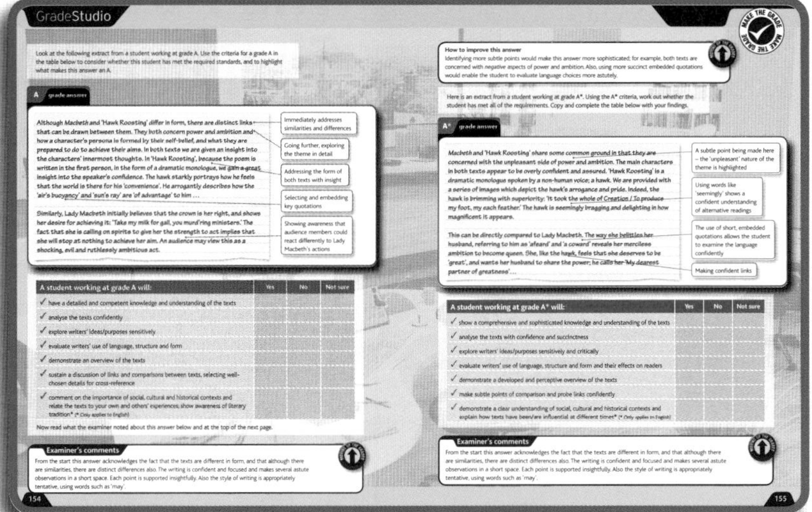

What additional resources are there?

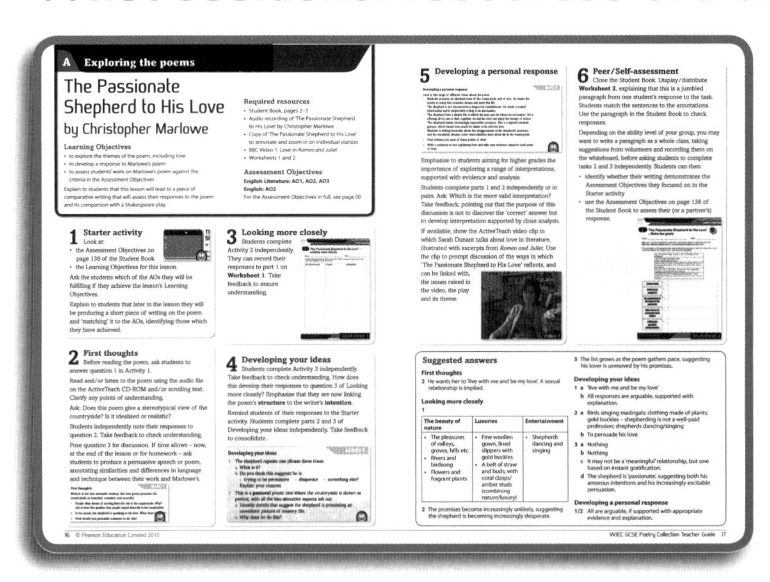

Teacher Guide

Full colour lesson plans can be found in the corresponding Heinemann Teacher Guide written by experienced author David Grant and WJEC examiner and teacher Sarah Basham. These lessons make use of and reference the BBC footage and other resources on the ActiveTeach CD-ROM.

ActiveTeach CD-ROM

The ActiveTeach CD-ROM is an on-screen version of the student book together with BBC footage and other assets including: grade improvement activities; audio recordings of each poem and worksheets. There is also an electronic version of the WJEC Poetry Collection so that each poem can be annotated and used in the classroom. Teachers can input their own resources and all of the worksheets can be customised.

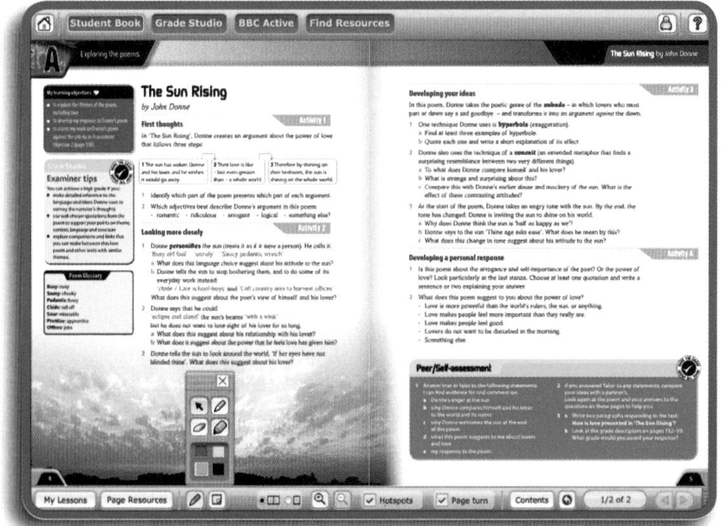

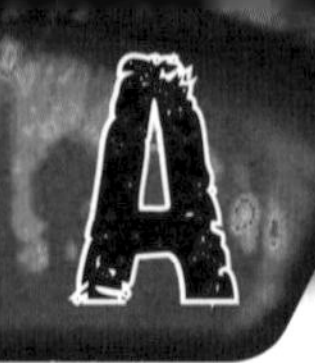

My learning objectives

- to explore the themes of the poem, including love
- to develop my response to Marlowe's poem
- to assess my work on Marlowe's poem against the criteria in Assessment Objective 2 (page 134).

GradeStudio

Examiner tips

MAKE THE GRADE

You can achieve a high grade if you:

- make detailed reference to the language and structure Marlowe uses to create the narrator's voice and the ways in which he tries to persuade his lover
- use well-chosen quotations from the poem to support your points on theme, content, language and structure
- explore comparisons and links that you can make between this love poem and other texts with similar themes.

Poem Glossary

Prove: test or try out
Grove: small group of trees
Madrigal: song
Kirtle: loose gown or long dress
Myrtle: evergreen plant
Amber: fossilised tree resin, often used in jewellery
Swain: young man

The Passionate Shepherd to His Love

by Christopher Marlowe

Activity 1

First thoughts

Written in the late sixteenth century, this love poem presents the countryside as beautiful, romantic and peaceful.

1 People often dream of moving from the city to the countryside. Why? List at least five qualities that people expect from life in the countryside.

2 In the poem, the shepherd is speaking to his love. What does he want?

3 How would you persuade someone to do this?

Activity 2

Looking more closely

1 List all the things that the shepherd offers his love. What *kinds* of things are they? Organise them under these headings, or choose your own:

The beauty of nature	Luxuries	Entertainment

2 **a** Which of the shepherd's promises would be easiest for him to keep?
b Which would be most difficult?
c What does this suggest about the shepherd and his promises?

3 Look at the *quantity* of things the shepherd offers as the poem progresses. What does this suggest about his love's response to these offers?

Activity 3

Developing your ideas

1 The shepherd repeats one phrase three times.
a What is it?
b Do you think this suggests he is:
• trying to be persuasive • desperate • something else?
Explain your reasons.

2 This is a **pastoral** poem: one where the countryside is shown as perfect, with all the less attractive aspects left out.
a Identify details that suggest the shepherd is presenting an unrealistic picture of country life.
b Why does he do this?

3 a What does the shepherd tell us about how he met his love, and about their past?
  b Apart from all the promises he makes, what does the shepherd say about how their relationship might develop in the future?
  c The shepherd promises 'pleasures' twice: in line 2 and line 19. What does this suggest about the relationship he is offering?
  d Look again at the poem's title. How does this add to your response to question 3c?

Activity 4

Developing a personal response

Look at this range of different views about the poem.

- Marlowe presents an idealised view of the countryside and of love. He wants the reader to enjoy this romantic dream and envy this life.
- The shepherd is not interested in a long-term commitment. He wants a sexual relationship and is desperately trying to be persuasive.
- The shepherd lives a simple life in which the past and the future do not matter. He is offering all he can so that, together, he and his love can enjoy the beauty of nature.
- The shepherd makes increasingly impossible promises. This is a typical romantic gesture, which shows how much he wants to be with his love.
- Marlowe is writing ironically about the exaggerations in the shepherd's promises, and the unrealistic dreams some town-dwellers have about life in the countryside.

1 Find evidence for each of these points of view.

2 Write a sentence or two explaining how and why your evidence supports each point of view.

Peer/Self-assessment

1 Read this paragraph, written in response to the task:
How does Marlowe present love in 'The Passionate Shepherd to His Love'?

2 Write a paragraph giving your own response to the task. Use the same structure as the paragraph on the right.

3 Annotate your paragraph, using the same notes as for the paragraph on the right. If you have forgotten to include anything in your paragraph, add it in.

4 Which criteria in Assessment Objective 2 on page 134 have you demonstrated in your paragraph?

A clear point

Evidence to support the point

The shepherd makes increasingly impossible promises. This is a typical romantic gesture, which shows how much he wants to be with his love:
'And I will make thee beds of roses
And a thousand fragrant posies'
By describing how he will bring the beauty of nature to his love, he is illustrating the beautiful, natural life she will enjoy if she comes to live with him. The poem is full of persuasive, romantic and often exaggerated language, such as 'fragrant' and 'a thousand', but the mention of 'beds' could be a clue to the shepherd's real intentions.

An explanation of the effect of the quotation

A different possible interpretation

Close focus on particular word choice

The Sun Rising

by John Donne

My learning objectives

- to explore the themes of the poem, including love
- to develop my response to Donne's poem
- to assess my work on Donne's poem against the criteria in Assessment Objective 2 (page 134).

Activity 1

First thoughts

In 'The Sun Rising', Donne creates an argument about the power of love that follows three steps:

1 The sun has woken Donne and his lover, and he wishes it would go away.

2 Their love is like – but even greater than – a whole world.

3 Therefore by shining on their bedroom, the sun is shining on the whole world.

1 Identify which part of the poem presents which part of each argument.

2 Which adjectives best describe Donne's argument in this poem:
- romantic • ridiculous • arrogant • logical • something else?

Activity 2

Looking more closely

1 Donne **personifies** the sun (treats it as if it were a person). He calls it:
'Busy old fool' 'unruly' 'Saucy pedantic wretch'
a What does this language choice suggest about his attitude to the sun?
b Donne tells the sun to stop bothering them, and to do some of its everyday work instead:
'chide / Late school-boys' and 'Call country ants to harvest offices'
What does this suggest about the poet's view of himself and his lover?

2 Donne says that he could:
'eclipse and cloud' the sun's beams 'with a wink'
but he does not want to lose sight of his lover for so long.
a What does this suggest about his relationship with his lover?
b What does it suggest about the power that he feels love has given him?

3 Donne tells the sun to look around the world, 'If her eyes have not blinded thine'. What does this suggest about his lover?

GradeStudio

Examiner tips

You can achieve a high grade if you:
- make detailed reference to the language and ideas Donne uses to convey the narrator's thoughts
- use well-chosen quotations from the poem to support your points on theme, content, language and structure
- explore comparisons and links that you can make between this love poem and other texts with similar themes.

Poem Glossary

Busy: nosy
Saucy: cheeky
Pedantic: fussy
Chide: tell off
Sour: miserable
Prentice: apprentice
Offices: jobs

Activity 3

Developing your ideas

In this poem, Donne takes the poetic genre of the **aubade** – in which lovers who must part at dawn say a sad goodbye – and transforms it into an argument *against* the dawn.

1 One technique Donne uses is **hyperbole** (exaggeration).
   a Find at least three examples of hyperbole.
   b Quote each one and write a short explanation of its effect.

2 Donne also uses the technique of a **conceit** (an extended metaphor that finds a surprising resemblance between two very different things).
   a To what does Donne compare himself and his lover?
   b What is strange and surprising about this?
   c Compare this with Donne's earlier abuse and mockery of the sun. What is the effect of these contrasting attitudes?

3 At the start of the poem, Donne takes an angry tone with the sun. By the end, the tone has changed: Donne is inviting the sun to shine on his world.
   a Why does Donne think the sun is 'half as happy as we'?
   b Donne says to the sun 'Thine age asks ease'. What does he mean by this?
   c What does this change in tone suggest about his attitude to the sun?

Activity 4

Developing a personal response

1 Is this poem about the arrogance and self-importance of the poet? Or the power of love? Look particularly at the last stanza. Choose at least one quotation and write a sentence or two explaining your answer.

2 What does this poem suggest to you about the power of love?
   - Love is more powerful than the world's rulers, the sun, or anything.
   - Love makes people feel more important than they really are.
   - Love makes people feel good.
   - Lovers do not want to be disturbed in the morning.
   - Something else.

Peer/Self-assessment

1 Answer true or false to the following statements. I can find evidence for and comment on:
   a Donne's anger at the sun
   b why Donne compares himself and his lover to the world and its rulers
   c why Donne welcomes the sun at the end of the poem
   d what this poem suggests to me about lovers and love
   e my response to the poem.

2 If you answered 'false' to any statements, compare your ideas with a partner's. Look again at the poem and your answers to the questions on these pages to help you.

3 a Write two paragraphs responding to the task: **How is love presented in 'The Sun Rising'?**
   b Look at the grade descriptors on pages 148–155. What grade would you award your response?

Cousin Kate

by Christina Rossetti

My learning objectives

- to explore the themes of the poem, including love
- to develop my response to Rossetti's poem
- to assess my work on Rossetti's poem against the criteria in Assessment Objective 2 (page 134).

GradeStudio

Examiner tips

You can achieve a high grade if you:

- make detailed reference to the ideas, language and structure Rossetti uses to convey the narrator's thoughts and viewpoint, and to create the poem's mood
- use well-chosen quotations from the poem to support your points on theme, content, language and structure
- explore comparisons and links that you can make between this poem of love and rejection and other texts with similar themes.

Poem Glossary

Flaxen: fair, blonde
Mean estate: a life of poverty
Coronet: small crown worn by a nobleman

Activity 1

First thoughts

1 'Cousin Kate' is a narrative poem – it tells a story. Place these key events in the order in which they appear in the poem.
- The narrator is a naive country girl.
- The narrator is seduced by a lord and becomes his lover.
- The narrator has a son.
- The narrator is rejected by the lord.
- The lord notices the narrator's cousin, Kate.
- The lord marries Kate.

2 The story is told in the first person ('I'). How might this affect the reader's reaction?

3 'Cousin Kate' was written more than 100 years ago. What does it tell you about attitudes to love, marriage and unmarried mothers at that time?

Activity 2

Looking more closely

1 Look at stanza 1. What evidence is there that the narrator was innocent before the lord seduced her? Why does she emphasise this at the beginning?

2 The narrator uses powerful language to describe her treatment and her reaction to it. For example:
'unclean' 'outcast' 'howl' 'spit'
   a Write a sentence or two commenting on the effect of each of these words in the poem.
   b How does this language choice contribute to the tone or mood of the poem?

3 An **oxymoron** is where two apparently contradictory words are placed together. For example, the narrator says the lord tempted her into a 'shameless shameful life'.
   a In what way was her life shameless?
   b In what way was it shameful?
   c How does this oxymoron express the narrator's confused feelings?

4 The narrator uses contrast throughout the poem. For example, she contrasts:
- her cottage with the lord's palace
- what the neighbours call her with what they call Kate.

   a What effect does each of these contrasts have?
   b Find two more examples of contrast and write a sentence or two commenting on their effect.

Activity 3

Developing your ideas

1 The narrator describes her treatment by the lord using two similes:
'He wore me like a silken knot,
He changed me like a glove'
What do these suggest about the lord's attitude to her?

2 The narrator describes herself as 'a cottage maiden / Hardened by sun and air'
Similarly, Kate is from 'mean estate', working 'among the rye'.
Why does this seem to add to the narrator's anger?

3 The narrator describes Kate's relationship to the lord as 'bound' with a ring. What does this word suggest about her feelings?

4 The poem has a rigid structure. Most of its language is simple and **monosyllabic** (in words of one syllable). What kind of voice do you imagine the narrator using as she tells her story in this way?

5 The last stanza introduces a different kind of love.
   a How would you describe the change of mood here?
   b How does the narrator describe her son?
   c How does she think that Kate and the lord feel about her son?
   d The narrator does not tell us about her child until the very end of the poem. Why might the writer have decided to structure the poem in this way?

Activity 4

Developing a personal response

1 The narrator says that, if she were in Kate's position, she would not have married the lord. Do you think this suggests:
- she is jealous of Kate
- she is glad to be rid of the lord
- she is judging the lord in the same way that society has judged her – and making a point about the different ways society judges men and women
- something else entirely?

2 a The lord is not named. How does this affect your response to him?
   b The narrator is not named either. How does this affect your response to her?

Peer/Self-assessment

1 Write two paragraphs responding to the task:
How is the love between the narrator and the lord presented in 'Cousin Kate'?

2 Look at the grade descriptors on pages 148–155. What grade would you award your response?

3 What could you change or add to improve your response? Use the grade descriptors to identify the two things most likely to improve your grade.

4 Redraft your answer, trying to make those changes.

5 Look again at the grade descriptors. Have you improved your grade?

My learning objectives

- to explore the themes of the poem, including love
- to develop my response to Shakespeare's poem
- to assess my work on Shakespeare's poem against the criteria in Assessment Objective 2 (page 134).

GradeStudio

Examiner tips

You can achieve a high grade if you:

- make detailed reference to the ideas, language and structure Shakespeare uses to convey the narrator's thoughts and create the poem's mood
- use well-chosen quotations from the poem to support your points on theme, content, language and structure
- explore comparisons and links that you can make between this love poem and other texts with similar themes.

Poem Glossary

Sonnet: poem of 14 lines with a regular rhyme pattern, often about love
Temperate: gentle, moderate
Lease: temporary ownership for an agreed price
Fair: beauty
Untrimm'd: unaltered

Sonnet 18

by William Shakespeare

Activity 1

First thoughts

1 In the opening line, the narrator wonders whether to compare 'thee' (you) to a summer's day. Who do you think the narrator is talking to?

2 a Look at the first two lines. Which does the narrator think is better: 'a summer's day' or 'thee'?
b In what ways is one better?

Activity 2

Looking more closely

1 The narrator goes on to list four ways in which a summer's day is not perfect.

'Rough winds do shake the darling buds of May,'
a How is summer described as less than perfect here?
b Why does the narrator describe the buds that grow in May as 'darling'?

'And summer's lease hath all too short a date:'
c What is the problem with the length of time that summer's 'lease' lasts?

'Sometime too hot the eye of heaven shines,'
d What is this metaphor referring to?
e What is the problem with summer in this line?

'And often is his gold complexion dimm'd;'
f Whose gold complexion is the narrator referring to?
g Compare this with the previous line. What is the problem now?

2 In lines 7–8, the narrator explores a problem with all of nature.
a In what way is nature changing throughout the year?
b In what way does nature never change (its 'course' is 'untrimm'd') from year to year?
c As years go by, what happens to beautiful people and things?

3 In line 9, the narrator moves back to praising his lover.
a Which word signals this change?
b How does the narrator suggest that his lover is different from summer and nature?

4 What are the 'lines' to which the narrator refers in line 12?

5 Look at the final two lines of the poem. To what does the word 'this' refer?

6 The poem has four sections. Match the section to the description:

Lines 1–2	explain how his poem will give his lover immortality
Lines 3–8	compare his lover to a summer's day
Lines 9–12	explore the ways in which summer and nature are not perfect
Lines 13–14	explore the ways in which his lover is above nature

Activity 3

Developing your ideas

1 The narrator addresses his lover directly by using the second person – 'thee'. What effect does this have on the reader?

2 Look at the nouns below. Which would complete the following sentence most accurately?
'Sonnet 18' is about ...
love nature summer beauty death life poetry decay
Rank them in order from most accurate to least accurate.

Activity 4

Developing a personal response

1 Shakespeare ends the poem by promising that it will preserve his lover for ever. How do you think Shakespeare wants his lover to respond to this?

2 Trace the mood of the poem by plotting each line on a mood graph like this one:

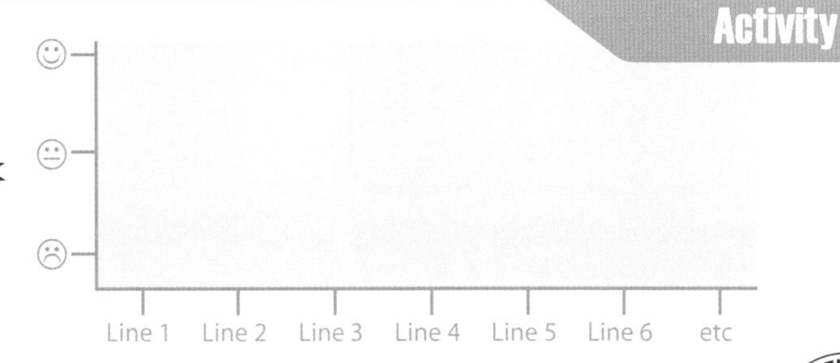

Peer/Self-assessment

MAKE THE GRADE

1 **Read this paragraph written in response to the task:**
How does Shakespeare present love in 'Sonnet 18'?

2 **Write a paragraph giving your own response to the task. Use the same structure as the paragraph above.**

3 **Annotate your paragraph using the same notes as the paragraph on the right. If you have forgotten to include anything, add it in.**

4 **Which criteria in Assessment Objective 2 on page 134 have you demonstrated in your paragraph?**

A clear point

Evidence to support the point

Shakespeare seems to praise the beauty of his lover, saying it will never fade:
'But thy eternal summer shall not fade'
This metaphor suggests that his lover has all the beauty of summer but, unlike summer, it will last forever. The word 'but' signals a shift in the mood of the poem, from the negative description of summer's inevitable decay, to the positive description of his lover's beauty lasting forever. The reader might expect Shakespeare to compare his lover to the beauty of summer flowers or weather. However, by emphasising the future, he suggests how long-lasting his love will be.

An explanation of the effect of the quotation

Explores the writer's intentions

Close focus on particular word choice

My learning objectives

- to explore the themes of the poem, including love
- to develop my response to Barrett Browning's poem
- to assess my work on Barrett Browning's poem against the criteria in Assessment Objective 2 (page 134).

GradeStudio

Examiner tips

You can achieve a high grade if you:

- make detailed reference to the ideas, language and structure Barrett Browning uses to convey her thoughts
- use well-chosen quotations from the poem to support your points on theme, content, language and structure
- explore comparisons and links that you can make between this love poem and other texts with similar themes.

Poem Glossary

Sonnet: poem of 14 lines with a regular rhyme pattern, often about love
Breadth: width
Ideal Grace: the grace of God
Quiet need: simple or basic need
Turn from: turn away from, avoid

Sonnet 43

by Elizabeth Barrett Browning

First thoughts

Activity 1

Elizabeth Barrett married fellow poet Robert Browning (to whom this sonnet is addressed) even though her father did not want her to ever marry. The couple went to live in Italy to escape his disapproval.

One phrase is repeated throughout the poem.

1. What is it?
2. How many times is it repeated?
3. What does this suggest about the poem's purpose?

Looking more closely

Activity 2

1. Barrett Browning tries to measure her love in lines 2 and 3.
   - **a** How does she measure it?
   - **b** What do these measurements suggest about her love?
2. Barrett Browning goes on to say her love is similar to ('to the level of') the basic needs of life ('every day's / Most quiet need').
   - **a** What are the basic requirements of life?
   - **b** If she needs his love to the same degree, what does this suggest about her love?
3. In lines 7, 8 and 9, Barrett Browning describes three ways in which she loves.
   - **a** What are they?
   - **b** Write a short comment on each, and on their combined effect: why did Barrett Browning choose them?
4. In lines 9–12, Barrett Browning compares the passion of her love with the passion of her religious faith in childhood, and of her 'old griefs' (perhaps the deaths of close relatives, as well as family problems over her marriage).
   - **a** What effect is created by the contrast between her love now and her past experiences?
   - **b** Barrett Browning compares her childhood feelings and thoughts with those she has now. What does this suggest about her love?
5. The poem concludes with two clear declarations of love.
   - **a** What does the triplet of 'breath, / Smiles, tears' suggest about her love?
   - **b** According to the final line, how long does Barrett Browning hope their love will last?
   - **c** What is the effect of this ending to the poem?

Activity 3

Developing your ideas

1 The poem starts with a question, which it goes on to answer. What effect do you think Barrett Browning intends this question to have on the reader?

2 a How successful is Barrett Browning in counting and measuring her love?
  b What does this suggest about her love?

3 Some of the things to which she compares her love are simple and mundane ('the level of every day's / Most quiet need') and some are complex and spiritual ('a love I seemed to lose / With my lost saints'). What effect does this contrast have?

4 Although much of the poem's language is positive, some is not.
  a Identify at least two examples of negative language.
  b What do you notice about their position in the poem? Are they at the beginning, middle or end?
  c Why do you think Barrett Browning chooses this position to introduce negative language?

5 Barrett Browning also uses alliteration throughout the poem.
  a How many examples can you spot?
  b What effect do they have?

Activity 4

Developing a personal response

1 In one part of the poem, Barrett Browning could be suggesting that she has lost her religious faith.
  a Can you find evidence to support this statement?
  b Can you find evidence to contradict it?

2 We might expect a love poem to praise its subject's beauty, kindness or other qualities.
  a What does the poem tell us about the physical appearance or positive qualities of Barrett Browning's lover?
  b Why do you think this is?

3 The poem explores many ways in which Barrett Browning loves. Are there any 'ways' she does not explore? Why do you think this might be?

Peer/Self-assessment

MAKE THE GRADE

1 Write two paragraphs responding to the task:
  How is love presented in 'Sonnet 43'?
2 Look at the grade descriptors on pages 148–155. What grade would you award your response?
3 What could you change or add to improve your response? Use the grade descriptors to identify the two things most likely to improve your grade.
4 Redraft your answer, trying to make those changes.
5 Look again at the grade descriptors. Have you improved your grade?

My learning objectives

- to explore the themes of the poem, including love
- to develop my response to Duffy's poem
- to assess my work on Duffy's poem against the criteria in Assessment Objective 2 (page 134).

GradeStudio

Examiner tips

You can achieve a high grade if you:
- make detailed reference to the ideas, language and structure Duffy uses to convey the narrator's thoughts
- use well-chosen quotations from the poem to support your points on theme, content, language and structure
- explore comparisons and links that you can make between this love poem and other texts with similar themes.

Valentine

by Carol Ann Duffy

First thoughts

Activity 1

1 What would you give as a Valentine's Day gift to someone you loved? A red rose, a satin heart, a cute card, or an onion?

2 Why do you think the poet has chosen to give an onion?

3 In the poem, Duffy makes surprising connections between love and an onion. For example:
'It will blind you with tears
like a lover.'
   a In what way can an onion blind you with tears?
   b In what ways can a lover blind you with tears? Try to think of at least two.

Looking more closely

Activity 2

1 Find at least three more connections Duffy makes between love and an onion. For each, write down:
   a a short quotation that shows the connection
   b a sentence or two explaining what it suggests about an onion and about love.

2 How would you describe Duffy's attitude to love? Is it positive, negative, or both? Choose quotations to support your answer.

Developing your ideas

Activity 3

1 Near the beginning of the poem, Duffy compares an onion to 'a moon wrapped in brown paper' which 'promises light' and is 'like the careful undressing of love'.
   a What connections can you see between an onion, love, the moon, brown paper and undressing? Copy the diagram below and write your ideas alongside each arrow.

An onion's outer skin is like brown paper

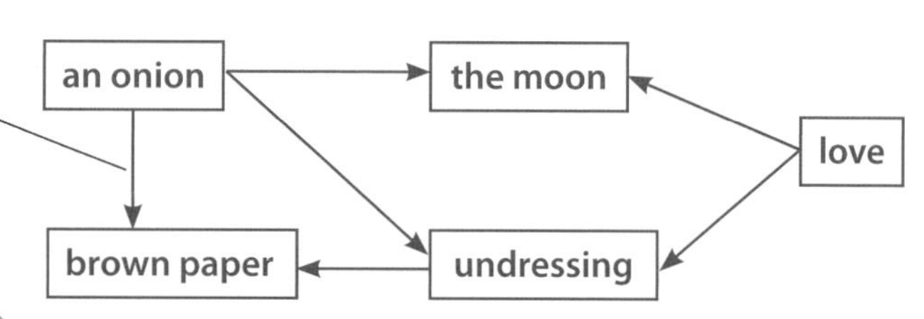

   b Why do you think Duffy uses this image to introduce the idea of an onion as a symbol of love?

2 Duffy chooses an intriguing combination of words to describe the experience of love:
'blind' 'grief' 'truthful' 'fierce' 'possessive' 'faithful' 'shrink' 'lethal' 'cling' 'knife'

Look at how each of them is used. Write a sentence or two about why you think Duffy chooses each one. For example:

> Describing a kiss as 'fierce' suggests it is very passionate. However, it also makes me think the relationship may be violent and soon over.

3 Three of the stanzas have only one line.
  a Can you make any connection between them?
  b What effect do they have?
  c The word 'lethal' is given a line to itself. What effect does this have?

4 Stanza 2 begins with a clear statement: 'I give you an onion.'
  a Who is Duffy talking to here – and throughout the poem?
  b What kind of language does she choose – complex or simple? Why do you think this is?

5 Duffy starts two stanzas with very short, blunt sentences: 'Here.' 'Take it.'
  a What do these lines suggest Duffy is doing?
  b What do they suggest about her lover's reaction?

Activity 4

Developing a personal response

1 What impressions does the poem give you of the writer's attitude to love, and to this particular relationship? Look at these different answers to the question:

Student A

> Duffy wants to write honestly about this relationship, and this is reflected in her decision to give her lover an onion. She chooses not to give an obvious, traditional gift but something that allows her to explore her true feelings.

Student B

> Duffy seems to have a negative attitude to love in 'Valentine'. Although she writes about 'fierce kisses' and being 'faithful', she adds the word 'possessive', turning two positives into a negative. In the end, she describes the 'platinum loops' of the onion shrinking to a wedding ring. The word 'shrinks' suggests that marriage is not a happy ending. She emphasises this point by immediately adding the word 'lethal'.

2 Which of these answers do you agree with most?
3 Look at the grade descriptors on pages 148–155. Which of these answers do you think would achieve the highest grade? Why?
4 Write a paragraph giving your own response to the question.

Peer/Self-assessment

1 Look again at the paragraph you have written in answer to the question above, and at the grade descriptors on pages 148–155. What grade would you award your answer?
2 What could you change or add to improve your answer? Use the grade descriptors to identify the two things most likely to improve your grade.
3 Redraft your answer, trying to make those changes.
4 Look once again at the grade descriptors. Have you improved your grade?

My learning objectives

- to explore the themes of the poem, including love
- to develop my response to Graves's poem
- to assess my work on Graves's poem against the criteria in Assessment Objective 2 (page 134).

GradeStudio

Examiner tips

You can achieve a high grade if you:

- make detailed reference to the language and structure Graves uses to tell this narrative
- use well-chosen quotations from the poem to support your points on theme, content, language and structure
- explore comparisons and links that you can make between this love poem and other texts with similar themes.

Poem Glossary

What ails you?: What is the matter with you?

A Frosty Night

by Robert Graves

Activity 1

First thoughts

1 'A Frosty Night' tells of a conversation between two characters. Who are they?

2 When does the conversation take place?

3 What has just happened to prompt this conversation?

4 Is the relationship between these two characters presented positively or negatively?

5 In this poem, two different kinds of love are competing for Alice's attention and loyalty. What kinds of love are they?

Activity 2

Looking more closely

1 Look again at the poem. Decide which character says which lines.

2 a Look again at the first three stanzas. In these, the mother speaks four sentences. What kind of sentences are they?
  b How do these sentences add to your understanding of the mother's personality?

3 a In the second line, the mother describes how Alice appears to be feeling. What does she say?
  b What does Alice claim has caused this?

4 Look again at stanza 2.
  a What is the mother doing?
  b What does this suggest about their relationship?
  c Alice is trying to write a letter. Who do you think she is writing to?

5 Alice's mother does not seem convinced by her explanation. She says that although it is cold outside, Alice was behaving as though birds were 'twittering / Through green boughs of June' and that she was skipping higher than 'all the lambs of May-day'.
  a How does Alice's mother know that she was behaving in this way?
  b What does this suggest about Alice's mother?
  c What is Alice's mother suggesting happened outside?
  d Why has the poet chosen to make a comparison between Alice's behaviour and things that happen in spring and summer?

6 In the final two lines of the poem, the mother confronts Alice with her final question.
  a What does Alice mean when she replies, 'Mother, let me go!'? Try to think of two different possible answers to this question.

Developing your ideas

Activity 3

1 Just before accusing Alice of being in love, her mother compares her daughter's appearance to both a ghost and an angel. What does this contrast suggest about love?

2 Can you identify any other places in which the writer has chosen to use contrast? What do they suggest about the experience of being in love?

3 Identify all the clues that lead Alice's mother to the conclusion that someone has said 'I love you' to her daughter.

4 Alice's mother obviously recognises the signs of a girl in love. What does this suggest about Alice's mother?

Developing a personal response

1 Different people respond to poems in different ways.
   a Choose some words from the list on the right – and add some of your own – to describe how you respond to:
      - the mother
      - Alice
      - their relationship.
   b How might a parent's view differ from yours? What would they say about:
      - the mother?
      - Alice?
      - their relationship?

caring	secretive
controlling	emotional
reckless	naive
romantic	interfering

Peer/Self-assessment

1 You are going to explore this question:
'A Frosty Night' explores the conflict between two kinds of love: parental and romantic. How does it present them?
Choose three quotations from those given below, and use them to write three paragraphs in which you:
- respond to the task
- comment on the effect of the writer's choice of language.

'Your eyes were frosted star-light;
Your heart, fire and snow.'

'Your feet were dancing, Alice,
Seemed to dance on air,'

'Mother, do not hold me so,
Let me write my letter.'

'Stars danced in the sky –
Not all the lambs of May-day
Skip so bold and high.'

'Alice, dear, what ails you,
Dazed and lost and shaken?'

'You looked a ghost or angel
In the star-light there.'

'Who was it said, "I love you"?'
'Mother, let me go!'

2 Which criteria in Assessment Objective 2 on page 134 have you demonstrated in your answer?

The Flea

by John Donne

My learning objectives

- to explore the themes of the poem, including love
- to develop my response to Donne's poem
- to assess my work on Donne's poem against the criteria in Assessment Objective 2 (page 134).

GradeStudio

Examiner tips

You can achieve a high grade if you:

- make detailed reference to the ideas, language and structure Donne uses to convey the narrator's thoughts and the ways in which he tries to persuade his lover
- use well-chosen quotations from the poem to support your points on theme, content, language and structure
- explore comparisons and links that you can make between this love poem and other texts with similar themes.

Poem Glossary

Mark: notice, look at
Maidenhead: virginity
Woo: seek someone's love
Stay: wait
Jet: black gemstone used for jewellery, also a symbol of mourning
Sacrilege: disrespect of a sacred or holy object
Yield: give in

Activity 1

First thoughts

1. What do you think of when you think about fleas? List some words.
2. 'The Flea' is a seduction poem: a man tries to persuade a woman to give up her virginity and sleep with him. Can you see any connections between the list of words you wrote and the poem's subject?

Activity 2

Looking more closely

1. The poem uses the second person 'thee' (you) and it is written as a one-sided dialogue – we don't hear the woman's responses. What effect does this create?
2. At the start of the poem, Donne asks us to look at this flea. What do you imagine him doing at this point?
3. In line 2, Donne complains that the woman is denying him. What is she denying him?
4. Donne compares himself, the woman and their relationship to the flea. What is he suggesting? Should he be taken seriously?
5. In stanza 2, the woman seems to threaten to kill the flea. Look carefully at the last three lines. What kind of language does he use to try to stop her?
6. In stanza 3, the woman has 'Purpled' her nail. What has she done? Do you think the reader is meant to find this funny?
7. Finally, Donne agrees that killing the flea has not weakened him or the woman, so its death is unimportant. How does he use this to make one last attempt to persuade her?

Activity 3

Developing your ideas

1. Donne's poem has its own strange logic. In which stanza does he present which arguments to make which points? Copy the notes below, matching the stanza numbers, arguments and points.

In stanza	he argues that	to make the point that
1	Their blood mingling in the flea is a kind of marriage and therefore she should not kill the flea	She will not damage anyone's honour if she has sex with him
2	Killing the flea hasn't hurt or weakened either of them	Having sex should cause no shame
3	Their blood mingling inside the flea is not a sin and has caused no shame	She should respect the 'marriage' they already have and show generosity to him

2 a What tone would you advise an actor giving a dramatic reading of the poem to use:
- cajoling
- aggressive
- humorous
- desperate
- something else?

You may decide that the tone changes at different points in the poem.

b Select a short quotation to support each adjective you choose.

3 Throughout the poem, Donne uses language with sexual undertones.

a Find some examples.

b How does this language contribute to the effect of the poem? Does it:
- make it clear exactly what Donne wants, without having to say it directly
- add humour
- help make his argument more persuasive
- something else?

Activity 4

Developing a personal response

1 a Why do you think Donne chooses something as insignificant as a flea to represent his subject, even though it is clearly important to the narrator?

b Using a flea as the central metaphor in a love poem seems extremely odd. In what ways is it an effective metaphor for a sexual relationship?

2 Do you think Donne's argument would persuade the woman? Why?

3 What do you think of the way he reverses his argument at the end?

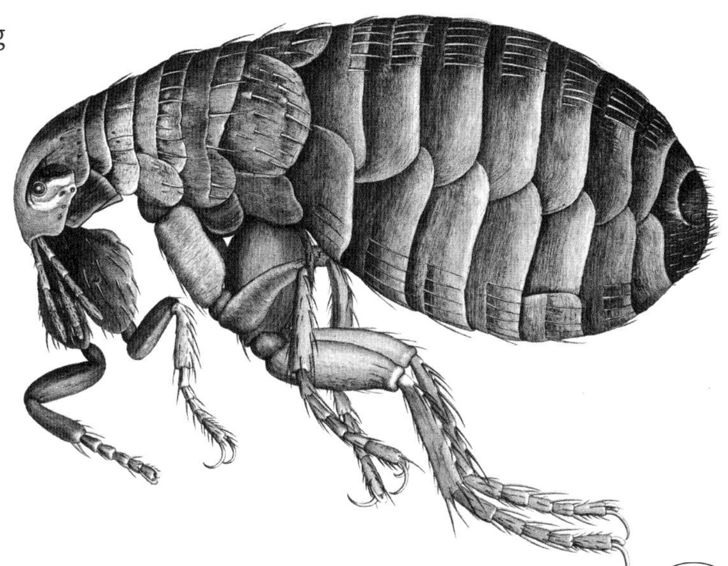

Peer/Self-assessment

MAKE THE GRADE

1 You are going to explore this question:
In 'The Flea', Donne explores his love relationship with a woman.
How does he present it?

Choose two of the quotations below and use them to write two paragraphs in which you:
- respond to the task
- comment on the effect of the writer's choices of imagery and language.

'Mark but this flea, and mark in this,
How little that which thou deny'st me is;'

'Yet this enjoys before it woo,
And pampered swells with one blood made of two,
And this, alas, is more than we would do.'

'This flea is you and I, and this
Our marriage bed,'

'Just so much honour, when thou yield'st to me,
Will waste, as this flea's death took life from thee.'

2 Which criteria in Assessment Objective 2 on page 134 have you demonstrated in your answer?

My learning objectives

- to explore the themes of the poem, including love
- to develop my response to Donne's poem
- to assess my work on Donne's poem against the criteria in Assessment Objective 2 (page 134).

GradeStudio

Examiner tips

You can achieve a high grade if you:

- make detailed reference to the ideas, language and structure Donne uses to convey the narrator's thoughts and viewpoint
- use well-chosen quotations from the poem to support your points on theme, content, language and structure
- explore comparisons and links that you can make between this poem about love and religion and other texts with similar themes.

Poem Glossary

Ravish: take by force or with violence
Whet: sharpen or stimulate
Head: head or source of a river
Dropsy: disease in which the body retains water and the sufferer is constantly thirsty
Woo: seek someone's love

Holy Sonnet 17

by John Donne

Activity 1

First thoughts

This poem was written shortly after Donne's wife died in childbirth.

1 What would you expect from a poem written under these circumstances?

2 Look at the language. What has his wife's death led Donne to think about? Is this a conventional love sonnet?

Activity 2

Looking more closely

1 The word 'death' does not appear in the poem. Donne simply says that the woman he loved has 'paid her last debt'. If life is a debt we must pay back, who do we owe it to?

2 Donne tells us that his wife's 'soul' has been 'early into heaven ravishèd'. Consider the words 'early' and 'ravishèd'. What does Donne's language choice suggest about his feelings regarding her death?

3 Donne says that the death of his wife, who was so close to God, has encouraged him – 'whet' his 'mind' – to seek God. He sums this up with a comparison: 'so streams do show the head'. What do you think he means? Refer to the Glossary opposite.

4 In the middle of the sonnet, in lines 7 and 8, Donne declares the problem he is wrestling with. As in the rest of the poem, he uses the second person 'thee' (you).
   a Who is Donne talking to?
   b What is the problem he is trying to solve?

5 In the last six lines, Donne tells God that he fears his love for his wife and for the things of this world will put God out of his mind.
   a Which three words does Donne use to sum up earthly love?
   b Which three words does he use to sum up heavenly love?
   c What effect is created by using these two 'patterns of three' to describe the two loves fighting within him?

Developing your ideas

Activity 3

1 The poem makes a number of references to water. What is Donne suggesting through the metaphor of water?

2 Look closely at this quotation:
'Wholly on heavenly things my mind is set.'
How would you describe Donne's tone as he addresses God in the first half of the poem, and in this quotation in particular?

3 Now look closely at this quotation:
'But why should I beg more love'
  a How would you describe Donne's tone as he addresses God in the second half of the poem, and in this quotation in particular?
  b In what way has the tone changed? Why?

4 Look at the language Donne uses to describe God's actions and feelings:
'ravishèd' 'woo' 'tender jealousy'
  a Would you expect to find these words in a religious poem? Where would you expect to find them?
  b What does this suggest about Donne's relationship with God?

Developing a personal response

Activity 4

1 This poem is both a love sonnet and a religious sonnet.
What is the effect of the conflict between these two subjects?

2 a Has Donne solved his problem by the end of the sonnet?
  b Why do you think Donne chooses to end the poem at this point?

Peer/Self-assessment

MAKE THE GRADE

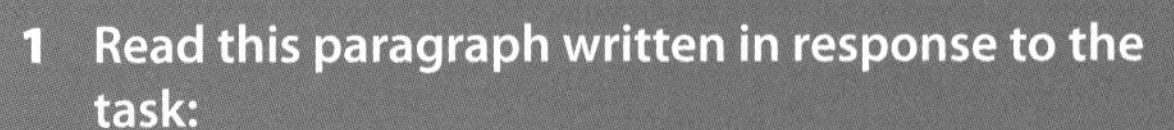

1 Read this paragraph written in response to the task:
How does 'Holy Sonnet 17' explore Donne's reaction to the death of his much-loved wife?

2 Write a paragraph giving your own response to the task. Use the same structure as the paragraph on the right.

3 Annotate your paragraph using the same notes as the paragraph on the right. If you have forgotten to include anything in your paragraph, add it in.

4 Which criteria in Assessment Objective 2 on page 134 have you demonstrated in your paragraph?

Evidence to support the point

A clear point

Donne expresses his feelings at his wife's death. He says that God:
'her soul early into heaven ravishèd'.
He clearly feels that his wife's life has been taken too soon. The choice of the word 'ravishèd' suggests Donne's intense anger at her death. It implies not only the violence of her death, but that Donne blames God for this brutal and intentional action. The shocking sexual overtones of the word almost suggest that Donne regards it as a crime.

An explanation of the effect of the quotation

How language reflects the poet's point of view

Close focus on particular word choice

My learning objectives

- to explore the themes of the poem, including parent/child relationships
- to develop my response to Harrison's poem
- to assess my work on Harrison's poem against the criteria in Assessment Objective 2 (page 134).

GradeStudio

MAKE THE GRADE

Examiner tips

You can achieve a high grade if you:

- make detailed reference to the language and structure Harrison uses to convey the narrator's thoughts
- use well-chosen quotations from the poem to support your points on theme, content, language and structure
- explore comparisons and links that you can make between this poem about parent/child relationships and other texts with similar themes.

Long Distance II

by Tony Harrison

First thoughts

Activity 1

1 The poem is spoken by a narrator. Who is the narrator, and what can you detect about him?

2 What is the narrator's attitude towards his father?

Looking more closely

Activity 2

1 Re-read the first two stanzas and make a note of what you find out about his father and his actions.

2 What do you think the relationship is like between the father and child in the first two stanzas? Explain how strong you think the relationship is and find evidence in the poem for this.

Plot this on a graph like the one below.

Strength of relationship

Time in the poem

3 Look at the last two stanzas. Do these suggest that the relationship is stronger, weaker or the same as you previously thought? Add your ideas to the graph, and select short quotations to support them.

4 Re-read the last stanza and consider why Harrison ends his poem this way. What point might he be trying to make about the son's relationship with his parents?

Developing your ideas

Activity 3

1 In this poem the actions of the characters are very important; they say more about how characters are feeling than their words. List the actions that the father takes, and then the son's, and comment on what they really mean.

The first one has been done for you:
'Dad kept her slippers warming by the gas'
What is he doing?

Here the father is pretending that the mother hasn't died; this is shown by the fact that he keeps her slippers, and that he has them warmed ready for her to put on, almost as if she has just popped out to the shops.

Why is it effective?

The fact that he keeps such everyday objects is moving because it shows he has not really come to terms with her death.

2 The poem has been written from a particular viewpoint. It is almost as if the narrator is chatting with us. In which lines do you think the viewpoint is most effective? Do you notice it changing at any point?

3 Many readers find the last stanza very moving. Discuss your feelings about it. Why do you think Harrison chooses to end the poem with the words: 'there's your name / and the disconnected number I still call.'

Activity 4

Developing a personal response

1 What have you learned about the narrator of the poem? How far can we trust his comments about his feelings?

2 One student said: 'This poem shows that we are more like our parents than we like to think.' How far do you agree that this statement is relevant to this poem?

Peer/Self-assessment

1 Read this paragraph written in response to the task:

How does Harrison present a parent/child relationship in 'Long Distance II'?

2 Write a paragraph giving your own response to the task. Use the same structure as the paragraph on the right.

3 Annotate your paragraph using the same notes as the paragraph on the right. If you have forgotten to include anything in your paragraph, add it in.

4 Which criteria in Assessment Objective 2 on page 134 have you demonstrated in your paragraph?

A clear point

Evidence to support the point

The poem is written from an adult's point of view. The narrator is reflecting on his father: 'You couldn't just drop in. You had to phone.' Harrison writes conversationally as if he is speaking to the reader; this is shown by the word 'you'. He appears to show some annoyance because his father expects calls and does not like his son to visit without giving him sufficient warning. The use of short sentences appears to reflect his impatience.

Close focus on the writer's choice of words

The idea is developed and shows the poet's point of view

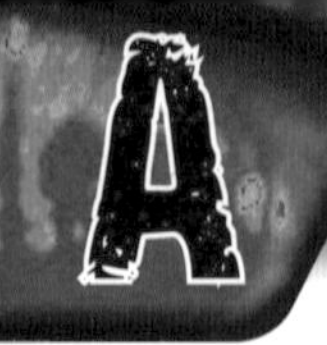

Catrin

by Gillian Clarke

My learning objectives

- to understand the themes of the poem, including parent/child relationships
- to develop my response to Clarke's poem
- to assess my work on Clarke's poem against the criteria in Assessment Objective 2 (page 134).

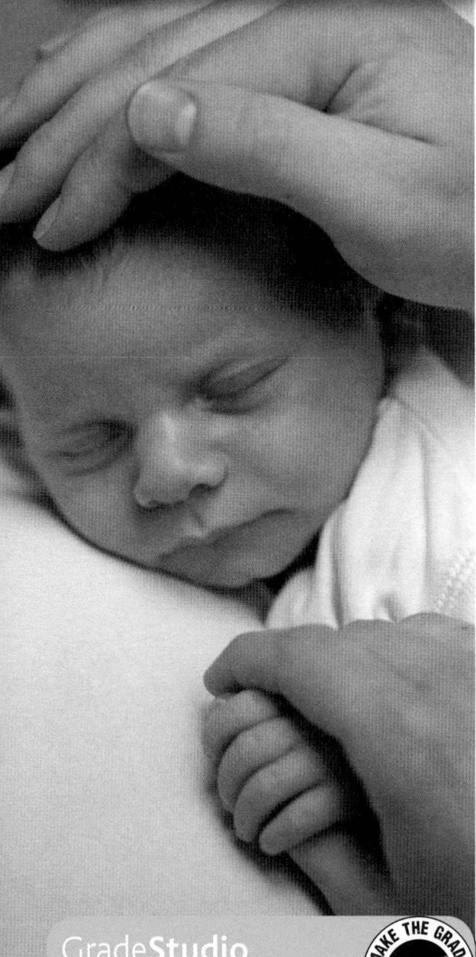

First thoughts

Activity 1

1 This poem is about the relationship between a mother and child. With a partner, jot down the positive and negative feelings a parent might have towards their child.

2 Look again at the poem. How would you explain the mother's attitude towards her daughter to someone who had not read it?

Looking more closely

Activity 2

1 Re-read stanza 1. It describes the birth and the hospital environment.
  a How does the poet describe the hospital?
  b How does the mother react when she is in pain?

2 In stanza 2 the poem shifts in time to the present. Find two words that show this.

3 Discuss the following lines with your partner:
  'Neither won nor lost the struggle
  In the glass tank clouded with feelings
  Which changed us both.'

  Write down three questions you would like to ask about these lines. Then discuss your questions with another pair.

4 Look carefully at the words used in the description of the young girl.
  'Still I am fighting
  You off, as you stand there
  With your straight, strong, long
  Brown hair and your rosy,
  Defiant glare'
  a How do you think the mother feels about her daughter now?
  b Pick one adjective and explain why you think it has been used to describe the girl. For example, why do you think the mother describes her daughter's hair in such detail?

Developing your ideas

Activity 3

1 Think about the poem as a whole. Students have made the following comments. Decide whether you disagree or agree with each, and find evidence to support your opinion.

Student A

'This poem shows a huge amount of pain and unhappiness. There do not seem to be any benefits in having a child.'

Student B

'This poem is really realistic. Clarke shows that parent/child relationships are often hostile.'

GradeStudio

MAKE THE GRADE

Examiner tips

You can achieve a high grade if you:

- make detailed reference to the language and structure Clarke uses to convey the narrator's thoughts
- use well-chosen quotations from the poem to support your points on theme, content, language and structure
- explore comparisons and links that you can make between this poem about parent/child relationships and other texts with similar themes.

Student C

'Clarke may dislike her daughter at times, but the poem shows that she really loves her.'

Student D

'The setting of the poem in the hospital makes for a really depressing mood.'

Student E

'This poem shows that a parent/child relationship has to be about compromise and meeting each other half way.'

2 The poet has used a particular structure and included various poetic devices. In pairs, discuss the following choices Clarke has made, and think about why she has written the poem in this way. The first has been done for you.

Feature of the poem	Its effect	Why it has been chosen
The poem is divided into two very different stanzas	This divides the poem into the past (giving birth) and the present (the ongoing conflict with her daughter)	It emphasises that the conflict with her daughter is continuing; it happened in the past, but is still taking place
The poet uses violent words such as 'Fierce confrontation', 'wild', 'shouted', 'fighting / You off'	These words make the narrator seem …	
Sometimes words are repeated: 'We want, we shouted'	This emphasises …	
The narrator addresses the daughter directly. She calls her 'you', rather than using the third person to refer to her	This has the effect of …	

Developing a personal response

Activity 4

1 How successful do you think Clarke has been in capturing the conflict between parents and children?

2 If Catrin were to write a reply to her mother, what aspects of her mother's behaviour do you think she might comment on? Find evidence from the poem. Write a few lines showing how the daughter might present her view of the incident.

Peer/Self-assessment

1 Write two paragraphs responding to the task:
How is the relationship between a mother and daughter presented in 'Catrin'?

2 Look at the grade descriptors on pages 148–155. What grade would you award your response?

3 What could you change or add to improve your response?
Use the grade descriptors to identify two things most likely to improve your grade.

4 Redraft your answer, trying to make those changes.

5 Look again at the grade descriptors. Have you improved your grade?

Follower

by Seamus Heaney

My learning objectives

- to explore the themes of the poem, including parent/child relationships
- to develop my response to Heaney's poem
- to assess my work on Heaney's poem against the criteria in Assessment Objective 2 (page 134).

GradeStudio

MAKE THE GRADE

Examiner tips

You can achieve a high grade if you:

- make detailed reference to the language and structure Heaney uses to convey the narrator's thoughts
- use well-chosen quotations from the poem to support your points on theme, content, language and structure
- explore comparisons and links that you can make between this poem about parent/child relationships and other texts with similar themes.

Activity 1

First thoughts

A description of a person practising a skill might say:

First of all he takes a sharp knife with a long edge and smoothes the surface of the cake. He then measures out the exact quantity of icing sugar and water, and carefully mixes them to produce a smooth, thick paste ...

Notice the types of words used to describe these actions. The word 'carefully' shows that the person pays attention to doing the task correctly. His actions are also described as being precise: words such as 'smoothes', 'measures,' and 'exact quantity' all indicate precision and care.

Now look at Heaney's poem. What actions is the father undertaking? What are the actions of the boy?

Activity 2

Looking more closely

1. Choose three lines that show the father hard at work. Copy them out.
2. Annotate your chosen lines. Pay attention to all the verbs (actions) and the descriptions of the father. Think about why Heaney selects these words and what impression he is trying to create. For example:

He only has to do this once to get the result he wants [single]

This suggests a very slight, but decisive action [pluck]

'with a single pluck
Of reins, the sweating team turned round'

This shows the hard work and effort being put in; it describes the horses, but could also describe the father, as he is part of the 'work team' [sweating]

3. Write a sentence that explains the effect of one of the words you have selected.

Poem Glossary

Furrow: long, narrow trench made by a plough
Sock: part of the plough that cuts the earth
Sod: surface layer of soil or grass
Headrig: border of the field where the plough turns

Activity 3

Developing your ideas

1 a Look carefully at how the narrator describes himself. How does he see his own skill?
  b What did he think of his father when he was young? How is this different from how he sees his father now?

2 Look carefully at the structure of this poem. Why do you think Heaney decided to end the poem with the description of the father in the present?

3 The narrator's attitude towards his father changes as the poem progresses. Some students have given the following reactions to the narrator's attitude.

Student A

'This poem celebrates parent/child relationships because it shows that parents are to be admired, and have their own skills.'

Student B

'This poem is depressing because his once-strong father is now acting like an annoying child. Old age has made him seem a pathetic figure to his adult son.'

Student C

'This poem is realistic because as children we want to be like our parents, but when we are adults we can see that they have weaknesses and failings.'

Student D

'We feel more sympathy for the child than the father, because his illusions about his father are shattered at the end of the poem.'

  a Decide which you agree with, and find evidence from the poem to support them.
  b Work in pairs to discuss each of these ideas. Could the same quotations be used to illustrate opposing points of view?

Activity 4

Developing a personal response

1 Why do you think Heaney called the poem 'Follower'? What alternative title can you suggest?

2 What impression do you get of the father's view of his child at the start of the poem, and then when he is an old man? What questions might you ask the narrator about his relationship with his father?

Peer/Self-assessment

1 **Answer true or false to the following statements:**
I can find evidence for and comment on:
  a the narrator's feelings towards his father when he is a child
  b the narrator's feelings towards his father when he is an adult
  c what this poem suggests to me about fathers and children
  d whether I think this poem has a happy or sad mood
  e how Heaney shows the skills the father has
  f my response to the poem.

2 **If you answered 'false' to any statements, compare your ideas with a partner's. Look again at the poem and your answers to the questions on these pages to help you.**

3 **a** Write two paragraphs responding to the task:
  How does Heaney present a father/son relationship in 'Follower'?
  b Look at the grade descriptors on pages 148–155. What grade would you award your response?

My learning objectives

- to explore the themes of the poem, including parent/child relationships
- to develop my response to Causley's poem
- to assess my work on Causley's poem against the criteria in Assessment Objective 2 (page 134).

GradeStudio

MAKE THE GRADE

Examiner tips

You can achieve a high grade if you:

- make detailed reference to the language and structure Causley uses to convey the narrator's thoughts
- use well-chosen quotations from the poem to support your points on theme, content, language and structure
- explore comparisons and links that you can make between this poem about parent/child relationships and other texts with similar themes.

What Has Happened to Lulu?

By Charles Causley

Activity 1

First thoughts

1 This poem is about a mystery. Write down three things you would like to ask about the situation. Compare your questions with a partner's. What seems to have happened?

2 Read the poem aloud. Try using different tones of voice to create a suitably unsettling mood. Are there particular words that would benefit from being emphasised?

Activity 2

Looking more closely

1 Who do you think the narrator of the poem is? What clues can you find to support your ideas?

2 What ideas do you have about the mother? Look at the words below and pick out two that seem most appropriate. You could use a dictionary to check your understanding. Make sure that you can support your ideas with evidence (quotations) from the text.

sympathetic	fearful	lonely	concerned	heartless
determined	spiteful	deceitful	remorseful	callous
cold-hearted	proud	uncaring	melodramatic	kind
guilty	worried	truthful	distressed	confused
caring	secretive	thoughtful		

3 What do you think has happened to Lulu? Support your ideas with short quotations from the text. Is there more than one possible interpretation of her disappearance?

Activity 3

Developing your ideas

1 This poem is a **ballad** (a type of poem that tells a story, using a particular form. It often repeats phrases, or whole stanzas).
   a What do you notice about the structure of this poem?
   b Why do you think Causley decided that the ballad form was the best for presenting his ideas?

2 Ballads are often spoken aloud as a form of story telling, and frequently relate tragic or mysterious events. They have a particular rhythm and rhyme scheme. Read the poem aloud with a partner. Think about the effect of the rhyme and rhythm. What do they add to the poem?

3 The writer has selected various techniques to put his ideas across. Match the writer's choices below to the intended effect.

Technique	Effect created
Use of questions	Builds up a clear picture in the reader's head, so they can imagine the scene
Highly visual descriptions, including precise details, e.g. 'circle on the dusty shelf / Where her money-box used to be'	Adds to the sense of mystery
Hints or forebodings of disaster, such as the hearing of voices 'In anger or in pain'	Emphasises uncertainty; also suggests that the truth is being deliberately hidden from the narrator
A narrative told from one particular viewpoint, relating only a few of the facts	Builds up tension and uncertainty about what really happened

Developing a personal response

Activity 4

1 Only two people are mentioned directly in the poem: Lulu and her mother. The narrator appears to be a younger child. Why do you think the poem considers only these two characters? Are there any questions you would like to ask about the wider family relationships?

2 Imagine you were asked to describe this poem and its effect on you in ten words. What would you say? Can you summarise the plot so easily? What effect does it have on you? Do you think this is what the writer intends?

Peer/Self-assessment

1 **Read this paragraph, written in response to the task:**
How does Causley present parents and children in 'What Has Happened to Lulu'?

2 **Write a paragraph giving your own response to the task. Use the same structure as the paragraph on the right.**

3 **Annotate your paragraph, using the same notes as for the paragraph on the right. If you have forgotten to include anything in your paragraph, add it in.**

4 **Which criteria in Assessment Objective 2 on page 134 have you demonstrated in your paragraph?**

A clear point

Evidence to support the point

Causley presents a relationship where there is clear conflict and turmoil:
'I heard somebody cry, mother,
In anger or in pain'.
Here the poet presents a mystery. Someone, presumably Lulu or the mother, has been crying late at night and there are obvious signs of a conflict. It is interesting that Causley does not make it clear why Lulu has left. He presents the questions through a younger sibling, which highlights the family's upheaval and unhappiness.

An explanation of the effect of the quotation

How it reflects the poet's point of view

Close focus on the writer's choice

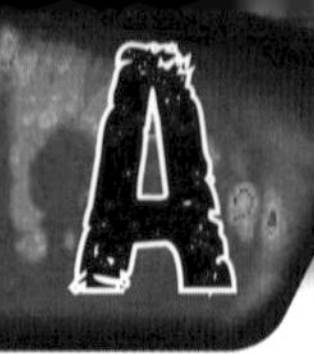

My learning objectives

- to explore the themes of the poem, including parent/child relationships
- to develop my response to Heaney's poem
- to assess my work on Heaney's poem against the criteria in Assessment Objective 2 (page 134).

GradeStudio

Examiner tips

You can achieve a high grade if you:

- make detailed reference to the language and structure Heaney uses to convey the narrator's thoughts
- use well-chosen quotations from the poem to support your points on theme, content, language and structure
- explore comparisons and links that you can make between this poem about parent/child relationships and other texts with similar themes.

Poem Glossary

Knelling: ringing, especially bells at a death or funeral
Stanched: the flow of blood stopped
Gaudy: very bright

Mid-Term Break

by Seamus Heaney

First thoughts

Activity 1

1 Heaney's brother really was killed in an accident. The poem shows the reaction of his family as he returns home from boarding school. Select three words or lines from the poem that show something is not right.

2 Which lines in the poem show a parent/child relationship?

Looking more closely

Activity 2

1 What impression do you get of the narrator of the poem?
   a What is his school like?
   b What do you know about his parents?
   c How does he react when people meet him? Why do you think this is?

2 Why do you think Heaney decided to write this poem from the perspective of the older brother? Why did he decide to use the first person, 'I'?

3 Heaney creates an uncertain and sombre atmosphere and uses imagery to describe his feelings, for example:
'Next morning I went up into the room. Snowdrops
And candles soothed the bedside'

The soft candlelight makes this seem a softer, kinder image.

You might associate this with mothers – 'soothing' or comforting young children. Here the harsh scene – the dead child in a coffin – is softened, creating a peaceful image.

'Snowdrops' sounds delicate, a small white flower with a drooping head. Why is this appropriate?

Explore the following lines in pairs.
'Counting bells knelling classes to a close.'
'With the corpse, stanched and bandaged by the nurses.'
'Paler now,
Wearing a poppy bruise on his left temple,'
'He lay in the four foot box as in his cot.'

Developing your ideas

Activity 3

1 In pairs, discuss the different reactions of people to the tragic death:
   - the neighbours
   - the mother
   - the father
   - the narrator.

   Select quotations to support your ideas.

2 The poem traces the narrator's journey from boarding school, until he finally sees his dead brother. Look carefully at the details he has included. Copy and complete the chart with ideas on why Heaney structured the poem this way.

Time	Place	Quotation	Your response	Effect
Waiting in the morning	School sick bay	'I sat all morning …'	A lonely, isolated image. We at first think he might be ill, before line 4 indicates something else is wrong	Makes the reader feel sorry for the narrator. He seems lonely, is away from his family and yet not comforted by anyone
		'Counting bells knelling classes to a close. / At two o'clock our neighbours drove me home'		
First entering the house				

Developing a personal response

Activity 4

1 This poem shows the death of a child through another child's viewpoint. How successfully do you think Heaney puts this across? Support your comments with ideas from the text.

2 Discuss with a partner how effective 'Mid-Term Break' is as a title. If you had to think of an alternative title, what would it be?

Peer/Self-assessment

1 **Read this paragraph, written in response to the task:**
How does Heaney present parent/child relationships in 'Mid-Term Break'?

2 **Write a paragraph giving your own response to the task. Use the same structure as the paragraph on the right.**

3 **Annotate your paragraph, using the same notes as for the paragraph on the right. If you have forgotten to include anything in your paragraph, add it in.**

4 **Which criteria in Assessment Objective 2 on page 134 have you demonstrated in your paragraph?**

Evidence to support the point

A clear point

Heaney shows the importance of parent/child relationships through the emotional reaction of both parents to their child's death:
'my mother held my hand
In hers and coughed out angry tearless sighs.'
There is a great sense of pain in the words used to describe the mother. She is not crying in a usual way – she seems too upset and almost angry. The word 'coughed' suggests the great pain and suffering she is holding back.

Close focus on the writer's choice of language

An explanation of the effect of the quotation

The Almond Tree

by Jon Stallworthy

My learning objectives

- to explore the themes of the poem, including parent/child relationships
- to develop my response to Stallworthy's poem
- to assess my work on Stallworthy's poem against the criteria in Assessment Objective 2 (page 134).

First thoughts

Activity 1

The poem describes the birth of a child, from the viewpoint of the father. Look carefully at the first two stanzas. What is the narrator's attitude towards this event? What happens to change it?

Looking more closely

Activity 2

1 The poem takes the reader on a rollercoaster journey of emotions beginning with the father's experiences on his journey to the hospital. Look at some of the key images below and decide why you think the poet uses them.

Key image	Emotion it suggests	Effect on the reader
On the journey to the hospital, 'the lights were green as peppermints.'	Happiness; everything seems to be going his way. The simile describes the traffic lights as bright green; peppermint seems a child-like, sweet image.	Makes us think that everything will go well for the narrator; a good omen creating a happy, cheerful mood.
'Trees of black iron broke into leaf'		
'The tower / held up its hand: the college / bells shook their blessing on his head.'		
'the tree / was waving, waving me / upstairs with a child's hands.'		
'the blood tide swung / me swung me to a room / whose walls shuddered / with the shuddering womb.'		

2 Look again at stanzas IV to VII and pick out the descriptions of the hospital. What do you notice about how Stallworthy has described this setting? How has he tried to make it vivid?

3 Re-read the reaction the narrator has on hearing that his son has Down's syndrome (stanza VI). How does the narrator feel at this stage? Pick one line that you think is the most effective in describing his suffering, and explain why.

Developing your ideas

Activity 3

1 The narrator's moods change radically in each stanza. Draw a mood graph (see page 9) to show his moods from the moment he starts his journey to the end of the poem. Plot for each stanza where you think his mood is, and select quotations to support your choices.

GradeStudio

Examiner tips

You can achieve a high grade if you:

- make detailed reference to the language and structure Stallworthy uses to convey the narrator's thoughts
- use well-chosen quotations from the poem to support your points on theme, content, language and structure
- explore comparisons and links that you can make between this poem about parent/child relationships and other texts with similar themes.

2 How effective is the title 'The Almond Tree'? What other title might be appropriate?

3 The image of the almond tree runs throughout the poem. Below is a mind map with one student's thoughts about this image and its uses. Discuss the student's findings, and add at least four ideas of your own.

Poem Glossary

Delta: mouth of a river
Mongol: old, now offensive, term for someone with Down's syndrome
Freight: cargo of a ship
Caul: membrane occasionally found covering a baby's head at birth

'The Almond Tree'

- Why 'almond'? Is the fact that almonds are bitter relevant? The experience is bitter/sweet for the narrator?
- It is described as beautiful and seems linked to the child as it has branches that wave 'with a child's hands'. Is it an image of a perfect child?
- The tree has fantastic blossoms – but it seems to lose them. Does this suggest loss?
- Why a tree? Is it linked with growth?

Activity 4

Developing a personal response

1 How do you think the narrator of the poem has changed as a result of his experience?

2 Jon Stallworthy comments that 'the poem was written in sections, each with a different stanza form, in an attempt to convey the different stages of the experience'. Choose two stanzas that have been written very differently and discuss with a partner how you think he has achieved this.

3 Some people have commented that there are parts of this poem that are similar to Ben Jonson's 'On My First Son' (page 34). Do you notice any similarities in any of the lines?

Peer/Self-assessment

1 Answer true or false to the following comments:
I can find evidence for and comment on:
   a the narrator's excitement about being a father
   b the disappointment and fear he feels about his child's condition
   c how he comes to terms with his situation
   d how the poem offers a sense of hope
   e my response to the poem.

2 If you answered 'false' to any statements, compare your ideas with a partner's. Look again at the poem and your answers to the questions on these pages to help you.

3 a Write two paragraphs responding to the task:
   How is fatherhood presented in 'The Almond Tree'?
   b Look again at the grade descriptors on pages 148–155. What grade would you award your response?

Prayer Before Birth

by Louis MacNeice

My learning objectives

- to explore the themes of the poem, including parent/child relationships
- to develop my response to MacNeice's poem
- to assess my work on MacNeice's poem against the criteria in Assessment Objective 2 (page 134).

GradeStudio

Examiner tips

You can achieve a high grade if you:

- make detailed reference to the language and structure MacNeice uses to convey the narrator's thoughts
- use well-chosen quotations from the poem to support your points on theme, content, language and structure
- explore comparisons and links you can make between this poem about parent/child relationships and other texts with similar themes.

Poem Glossary

Engendered: caused
Bureaucrats: government officials
Hector: bully
Dragoon: force
Automaton: person who acts like a machine
Dissipate: waste or scatter

Activity 1

First thoughts

1 List the fears someone might have for a baby entering the world today.

2 The poem has been written with a particular narrative voice. Who is the narrator? Why do you think MacNeice decided to write from this particular viewpoint?

Activity 2

Looking more closely

1 Read the poem aloud to yourself a few times. Experiment with different ways of reading it. What tone works best? Do you think particular words should be emphasised?

2 The poem is called 'Prayer Before Birth'. What do you notice that makes it seem like a prayer? Can you find examples of religious and archaic (old-fashioned) language? Why do you think MacNeice decided to echo a prayer?

3 Re-read stanzas 2, 3 and 4. The voice of the child seems to demand many things. Are the following statements true or false? Use evidence from the poem to support your answer.

The narrator wants:

- to live in nice surroundings
- to be given good guidance
- to be protected from the evil in the world.
- to be given a religious purpose
- to have great wealth

4 Every stanza begins with a different type of plea, and each lists many concerns. Why do you think the poet included such a range of dangers, needs and temptations?

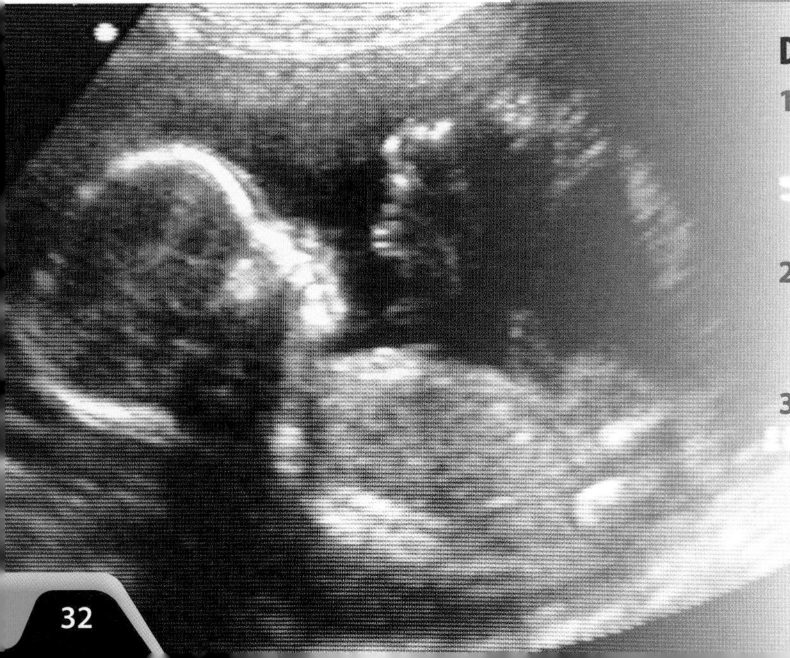

Activity 3

Developing your ideas

1 Many of the ideas in this poem are striking. Pick out three lines that you find particularly dramatic, and explain how the poet has created this effect.

2 The poem makes many references to the senses. Find three examples and explain how these add impact to the poem.

3 The poet uses a range of images to build up a picture in the reader's mind. Explore some of these by copying and completing the table on the next page.

Image	What it means	Why the language is effective
'bloodsucking bat'	A horrible creature – perhaps a child's fear, rather than real	The alliteration of the 'b' sound makes it forceful. The description 'bloodsucking' makes it sound dangerous
'club-footed ghoul'		
'a white light / in the back of my mind'		
'mountains / frown at me'		
'make me a cog in a machine'		

4 This poem does not make a direct reference to parents, although it does refer to other people and society. It was written during the Second World War. Does this seem relevant to the concerns of the poem?

5 The last lines are very dramatic and some readers find them shocking:
'Let them not make me a stone and let them not spill me.
Otherwise kill me.'

Do you think it is an effective conclusion to the poem? Give reasons for your answer.

Activity 4

Developing a personal response

1 The unborn child is not given a particular identity or even a sex in the poem. Why do you think MacNeice has made the child anonymous?

2 Some people find this a disturbing poem. How do you respond to it? Use examples from the poem to support your ideas.

Peer/Self-assessment

1 **Read this paragraph, written in response to the task:**
How does MacNeice present childhood in the poem 'Prayer Before Birth'?

2 **Write a paragraph giving your own response to the task. Use the same structure as the one on the right.**

3 **Annotate your paragraph using the same notes as for the paragraph on the right. If you have forgotten to include anything in your paragraph, add it in.**

4 **Which criteria in Assessment Objective 2 on page 134 have you demonstrated in your paragraph?**

Evidence to support the point

A clear point

The narrator speaks directly and dramatically to the reader about life:
'I am not yet born; O fill me
With strength against those who would freeze my humanity'.
Here the narrator speaks directly to the reader, using the powerful first person. The words sound almost like a prayer, with the use of 'O' urging the reader to help support the unborn child in the face of terrible hostility. It seems that the child needs defending against a very difficult and harmful world.

An explanation of the effect of the quotation

How it reflects the poet's point of view

Close focus on the writer's choice

On My First Son

by Ben Jonson

My learning objectives 

- to explore the themes of the poem, including parent/child relationships
- to develop my response to Jonson's poem
- to assess my work on Jonson's poem against the criteria in Assessment Objective 2 (page 134).

GradeStudio

Examiner tips

You can achieve a high grade if you:

- make detailed reference to the language and structure Jonson uses to convey the narrator's thoughts
- use well-chosen quotations from the poem to support your ideas on theme, content, language and structure
- explore comparisons and links that you can make between this poem about parent/child relationships and other texts with similar themes.

Poem Glossary

Thou wert: you were
Exacted: demanded
'Scaped: escaped
Henceforth: from now on

First thoughts

Activity 1

The poem opens with the line:
'Farewell, thou child of my right hand, and joy!'

In pairs, think of three questions you would like to ask the person speaking this line. For example: 'Why is the parent saying goodbye?'

Looking more closely

Activity 2

1 This poem was written in the seventeenth century. Look at the following words from the poem. Discuss their meaning with a partner, using a dictionary if necessary.
'farewell' 'joy' 'sin' 'hope' 'loved boy' 'pay' 'fate' 'lose all' 'father' 'lament' 'envy' 'flesh's rage' 'misery' 'rest' 'soft peace' 'vows' 'like'

Draw a bar like the one below and arrange the above words from the poem along it, so that the words with the most positive associations are on the left and the most negative ones are on the right. Explain your reasons for placing the words in the way you do.

Positive ←——— Neutral ———→ Negative

2 Jonson uses vocabulary associated with payment, love, pain and religion. Why do you think he chooses words connected with such contrasting ideas?

Developing your ideas

Activity 3

1 In pairs, read the poem aloud. Think about an appropriate tone of voice. Does the poem suit a particular tone, such as proud, sorrowful, fearful, resigned, hopeful?

2 Discuss the following statements and rank them in order, with the one you most agree with first. Find a quotation to support your ideas.

Ben Jonson feels:

- angry at his son's death
- his son has escaped the harsh world
- God is in control of the world
- his son is precious
- he should be dead, not his son
- he expected too much from his son
- proud of his skill in writing poetry.

Developing a personal response

Activity 4

1. Ben Jonson really did lose a seven-year-old son. In the seventeenth century, a large number of children died young. What evidence can you find in the poem about why Jonson might have written it?
2. The poem is written in rhyming couplets. Look at lines 3–4 as an example:
   'Seven years thou wert lent to me, and I thee pay,
   Exacted by thy fate, on the just day.'
   Why do you think Jonson connects the ideas of 'pay' and 'day'?
3. The punctuation is important in this poem. Look at the following line:
   'Oh, could I lose all father now!'
   Here the comma after the exclamation 'Oh' creates a slight pause that signals his anguish and pain. The exclamation mark emphasises his suffering.

   If you look at the full line in the poem, you will see that the sense runs on to the next line, as if the emotion cannot be contained and must spill over.

   Choose two other lines from the poem and discuss the effect of their punctuation.

Peer/Self-assessment

MAKE THE GRADE

1. Read this paragraph, written in response to the task:
   How does Jonson present the loss of a son in 'On My First Son'?
2. Write a paragraph giving your own response to the task. Use the same structure as the paragraph opposite.
3. Annotate your paragraph using the same notes as for the paragraph above. If you have forgotten to include anything in your paragraph, add it in.
4. Which criteria in Assessment Objective 2 on page 134 have you demonstrated in your paragraph?

Evidence to support the point

A clear point

This poem shows Jonson's pain and suffering. This is shown by the words 'loved boy', which are very simple but show his sincere feelings for his son. The fact that they are written so simply makes these words very moving. They also show the simple but overwhelming love the poet has for his son.

Close focus on the writer's choice of words

How it reflects the poet's point of view

An explanation of the effect of the quotation

My Grandmother

by Elizabeth Jennings

My learning objectives

- to explore the themes of the poem, including parent/child relationships
- to develop my response to Jennings's poem
- to assess my work on Jennings's poem against the criteria in Assessment Objective 2 (page 134).

GradeStudio

Examiner tips

You can achieve a high grade if you:

- make detailed reference to the language and structure Jennings uses to convey the narrator's thoughts
- use well-chosen quotations from the poem to support your points on theme, content, language and structure
- explore comparisons and links that you can make between this poem about parent/child relationships and other texts with similar themes.

Activity 1

First thoughts

1 Look at the following lines from the poem:
'And when she died I felt no grief at all,
Only the guilt of what I once refused.'

In pairs, think of three questions you would like to ask about these lines. For example: 'Why does the narrator not feel grief for the loss of her grandmother?'

2 Discuss your questions with another pair. What other information would you like to know?

Activity 2

Looking more closely

1 Many objects are mentioned in this poem. Think about why these have been selected, and what they might tell you about the characters in the poem.

2 In the first line, the antique shop is described as being almost like a person (**personification**). Explain why you think the shop is so important in this poem.

3 We don't find out very much about the grandmother. Look carefully at the poem again then copy and complete the table below.

What we think is true	Quotation to support this	What this means	Why the word choice is important	What we don't know
The grandmother does not have a close relationship with her grandchild	'And when she died I felt no grief at all'	The child is not really sad or sorry about her death	The words 'no' and 'at all' emphasise the absence of feeling	Is she trying to make herself feel better for refusing to go out with her grandmother? Does she have a good reason for not loving her grandmother? Was the grandmother unkind to her?
	'things she never used / But needed'			
	'She kept an antique shop – or it kept her.'			

4 The poem uses many descriptive words that appeal to the senses. Choose two examples and write a sentence about the effect of each. For example:

> The furniture is described as 'heavy'. This means you can imagine it being very old-fashioned and large.

Poem Glossary

Apostle spoons: silver spoons with images of Jesus Christ's disciples on the handles
Salvers: plates

Developing your ideas

Activity 3

1 Poems often have a particular mood or atmosphere. What sort of feeling do you think this poem captures? Below are some words used to describe its mood. In pairs, discuss which ones you think are the most appropriate.

happy solemn regretful disappointed guilty tragic
melancholy joyful tender wistful carefree disturbing
thoughtful unhappy angry controlled

2 This poem is written after the grandmother has died. It also describes her being in the antique shop, her increasing age, and then her death. Why do you think the poet chooses to describe the different stages of her life?

Developing a personal response

Activity 4

Look at the two opinions about the poem expressed below. Which one do you agree with most? Support your ideas with quotations.

Student A

This poem is really moving because the grandmother seems to have no love or affection in her life, just objects. The poem is mainly about the importance of the shop to her.

Student B

I disagree. This poem is all about emotions and relationships. The granddaughter feels terrible guilt because she once rejected her grandmother. The grandmother is also seen as a person who has trouble expressing love.

Peer/Self-assessment

MAKE THE GRADE

1 You are going to discuss this question:

'My Grandmother' explores the different feelings the narrator has towards her grandmother. How does the poet present these feelings?

Choose three of the quotations below, and use them to write three paragraphs in which you:

- respond to the task
- comment on the effect of the writer's choice of language.

'She kept an antique shop – or it kept her.'

'It was perhaps a wish not to be used
Like antique objects.'

'She watched her own reflection in the brass'

'Though she never said
That she was hurt,'

'Polish was all, there was no need of love.'

'The smell of absences where shadows come
That can't be polished.'

'I still could feel the guilt
Of that refusal,'

'things she never used
But needed'

'There was nothing then
To give her own reflection back again.'

2 Which criteria in Assessment Objective 2 on page 134 have you demonstrated in your answer?

My Heart is Like a Withered Nut!

by Caroline Norton

My learning objectives

- to explore the themes of the poem, including youth and age
- to develop my response to Norton's poem
- to assess my work on Norton's poem against the criteria in Assessment Objective 2 (page 134).

GradeStudio

Examiner tips

You can achieve a high grade if you:

- make detailed reference to the language and structure Norton uses to convey the narrator's thoughts and create the poem's mood
- use well-chosen quotations from the poem to support your points on theme, content, language and structure
- explore comparisons and links that you can make between this poem about youth and age and other texts with similar themes.

Poem Glossary

Comely: attractive
Hue: colour
Verdant: green and lush

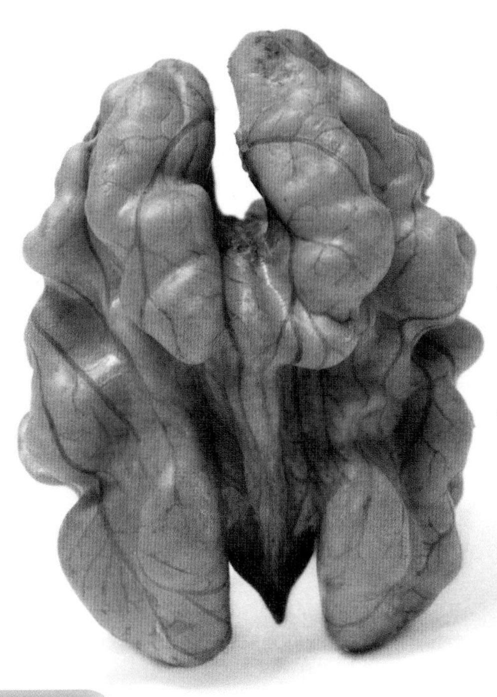

Activity 1

First thoughts

1 a How is the narrator's heart at the time of writing the poem?
  b Pick out at least three clues that tell you this.

2 a How was the narrator's heart in the past?
  b Pick out at least three clues that tell you this.
  c What is the basic contrast for the narrator between the experience of youth and that of age?

Activity 2

Looking more closely

1 In stanza 1, the narrator compares her heart to a withered nut. She says it is rattling in its hollow shell.
  a What do you think she means?
  b What has caused this?

2 The narrator goes on to write about the way that hopes and dreams filled her heart when 'Life's spring of glory met my view'.
  a What do you think 'Life's spring of glory' is?
  b When do you think it comes into view?

3 The narrator of the poem is clearly unhappy – but at the end of stanza 1, she says she does not think her heart will ever swell with joy *or* pain. What does this suggest about the state of her heart?

4 In stanza 2, the narrator writes:
  'Each light-toned voice once cleared my brow,
  Each gentle breeze once shook the tree
  Where hung the sun-lit fruit'
  a What effect did each 'light-toned voice' have on the narrator?
  b What is the connection between these voices and the breeze?
  c How does the way Norton writes these lines emphasise the connection?

5 In stanza 3, the narrator writes about 'misfortune's blast', which has affected her heart. How does this develop an image used earlier in the poem?

6 a Make a list of everything the narrator uses to describe her emotional states. You could begin with:
  - A withered nut
  - A hollow shell
  - A spring

  b What links all the things in your list?
  c Can you find any other examples of language that fit with this theme?
  d Why do you think the narrator chooses this theme for the extended metaphor that runs through the poem?

Developing your ideas

Activity 3

1 Each of the poem's stanzas has the same opening line. What is the effect of this repetition?

2 The words 'once' 'but' and 'now' are also used frequently in the poem. Why?

3 How would you describe the narrator's voice and the mood of poem as it progresses?
   a Track how it changes by completing a mood graph like the one on the right.
   b Now annotate your graph showing:
      - which lines describe the narrator's mood now, in the present
      - which lines describe her mood in the past.

   What do you notice?

Ecstatic								
Overjoyed								
Thrilled								
Pleased								
Happy								
Sad								
Upset								
Bitter								
Depressed								
Despairing								
Line number	1	2	3	4	(continued)			

4 a What do you think has happened to the narrator to cause this change of mood?
   b The narrator gives no detailed explanation. What effect does this have?

Developing a personal response

Activity 4

Look at the following range of different responses to the task:

How does Norton present the narrator's emotional state in youth and age in 'My Heart is Like a Withered Nut!'?

- The narrator uses extended natural imagery to describe the change in her heart.
- The narrator constantly compares the past with the present.
- There is no relief in the mood of the poem: even the joy of the past emphasises the misery of the present.

Turn each of these responses into point-evidence-explanation paragraphs by:

- finding evidence for each response
- adding a sentence or two explaining how and why your evidence supports each response.

Peer/Self-assessment

1 Look at your answer to Activity 4 above, and at the grade descriptors on pages 148–155. What grade would you award your answer?

2 What could you change or add to improve your response? Use the grade descriptors to identify the two things most likely to improve your grade.

3 Redraft your answer, trying to make those changes.

4 Look again at the grade descriptors. Have you improved your grade?

My learning objectives

- to explore the themes of the poem, including old age
- to develop my response to Hughes's poem
- to assess my work on Hughes's poem against the criteria in Assessment Objective 2 (page 134).

Grade**Studio**

Examiner tips

You can achieve a high grade if you:

- make detailed reference to the ideas, language and structure Hughes uses to convey the narrator's thoughts
- use well-chosen quotations from the poem to support your points on theme, content, language and structure
- explore comparisons and links that you can make between this poem about old age and other texts with similar themes.

Poem Glossary

Embers: glowing remains of a fire
Amnesia: loss of memory

Old Age Gets Up

by Ted Hughes

Activity 1

First thoughts

The poem describes an elderly person.

1. Where do you think this person is?
2. Describe the picture created in your mind as you read. Identify the words that create this.

Activity 2

Looking more closely

1. Much of the poem focuses on the elderly person's mind. Select quotations that show:
   - physical actions
   - the person's physical appearance.

   What do your quotations suggest about the elderly person?
2. The poem opens with an image of a fire.
   a. What is the connection between the person and this fire?
   b. Why would someone stir the ashes, embers and sticks of a fire?
3. In lines 4 and 5, we are told that this person's thoughts 'collapse / At the first touch of attention'. Why is this?
4. In lines 6–8, Hughes describes the light at the window.
   a. What do these lines suggest about the person's average day?
   b. Which words suggest this? Write a sentence or two explaining your answer.
5. In lines 11–12, Hughes writes about 'the blurred accident / Of having lived'.
   a. What is this accident? Why has it numbed the elderly person?
   b. Hughes builds on the description of an accident, calling it the 'fatal, real injury / Under the amnesia'. What is he suggesting?
6. a. In lines 14–16, what has happened to the elderly person's words?
   b. Why is the person looking for words?
   c. Why are they like flies? Try to think of at least three reasons.
7. In line 18, Hughes describes the person as 'Heavily dosed with death's night'. Choose three words from this quotation. What does each suggest?

Activity 3

Developing your ideas

1. Look at the table on the next page. Which of the poem's structural features do you think contribute to which effect?

Structural feature	Effect
Lines vary in length – one has only one word	Reflects the pace and progression of an elderly person's collapsing thoughts
No regular rhyme	Creates a series of disconnected observations
No regular rhythm	Reflects the physical struggle of old age
Irregular stanzas	
Little punctuation	Creates a sense of time steadily passing
Enjambment (lines run on to the next without punctuation)	

2 a Identify and comment on three images that suggest fragility and weakness.
b Look at the image that ends the poem:
'Pulls its pieces together
Loosely tucks in its shirt'
What does this suggest about the body and clothing of the elderly person?

Activity 4

Developing a personal response

1 a How do you think Hughes wants the reader to respond to the poem?
b What is *your* response? Select your answer from the list on the right – or add your own ideas. Choose evidence from the poem to support your answers.

- Sympathy
- Pity
- Fear
- Revulsion
- Anger
- Sadness
- Indifference

2 Hughes refers to the subject of the poem as 'it'. Does this suggest:
- Hughes is personifying old age, not writing about one elderly person
- Hughes is dehumanising an elderly person
- something else?

Support your answer with evidence and explain why you think Hughes chooses to do this.

Peer/Self-assessment

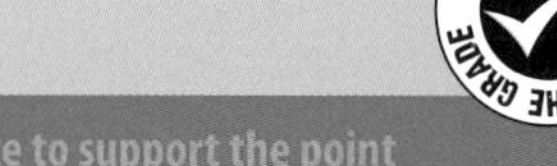

1 **Read this paragraph, written in response to the task:**
How does Hughes present old age in 'Old Age Gets Up'?
2 **Write a paragraph giving your own response to the task. Use the same structure as the paragraph on the right.**
3 **Annotate your paragraph using the same notes as the paragraph on the right. If you have forgotten to include anything in your paragraph, add it in.**
4 **Which criteria in Assessment Objective 2 on page 134 have you demonstrated in your paragraph?**

A clear point

Evidence to support the point

Hughes describes the window frame in the elderly person's room:
'A scaffold in space, for eyes to lean on'.
This suggests the frailty of the person. The word 'scaffold' implies not only that it is supporting the person physically, but it is the framework on which the person's day is built. It suggests that the elderly person spends all day looking out the window, and physical frailty has left the person nothing to do but stare into space.

An explanation of the effect of the quotation

How language reflects the poet's point of view

Close focus on particular word choice

My learning objectives

- to explore the themes of the poem, including youth and age
- to develop my response to Pugh's poem
- to assess my work on Pugh's poem against the criteria in Assessment Objective 2 (page 134).

GradeStudio

Examiner tips

You can achieve a high grade if you:

- make detailed reference to the language and structure Pugh uses to convey the narrator's thoughts and create the poem's mood
- use well-chosen quotations from the poem to support your points on theme, content, language and structure
- explore comparisons and links that you can make between this poem about youth and age and other texts with similar themes.

Sweet 18

by Sheenagh Pugh

First thoughts

Activity 1

1 Who are the characters in the poem? What clues tell you this?

2 One of these characters is young. At the beginning, the narrator gives brief details of this young man's physical appearance.
  a What are these?
  b What do they suggest about the character of the young man, and about being young?

Looking more closely

Activity 2

1 In the middle of the poem, the narrator compares the youth to glass, snow, and a blank canvas.
  a In each case, what is the narrator tempted to do?
  b What do all three comparisons have in common?
  c What do they suggest about how the poem might end?
  d What effect do you think Pugh wants these comparisons to have on the reader?

2 The narrator then uses an extended metaphor to compare the youth with a meal, describing how she would taste it and 'would leave nothing'. What does this suggest?

3 The narrator's final comparison describes the youth as a 'young sapling' and herself as
'ivy, resting / her lameness'
What does this suggest about the relationship the narrator imagines with the young man?

4 Look at the last two words. Why does the narrator end with these?

Developing your ideas

Activity 3

1 The narrator writes as if talking to the youth: the first word is 'You'. What effect does this direct address have?

2 Near the beginning, the narrator says:
'It stands to reason I must want you to stay
like this: who could wish to make away
such innocence, such perfection?'
Near the end, however, she appears to be threatening destruction:
'I would leave nothing.'
  a What do you think is the meaning of this contrast?
  b What does this suggest about the narrator's 'reason'?

3 Re-read the last line of the poem. It is ambiguous; it can be interpreted in a number of ways. Do you think:
- The narrator is asking the youth to give her a glass of light? What would this suggest?
- The narrator is addressing the youth as 'glass of light'? What would this suggest?
- Something else entirely?

4 Why do you think Pugh chose this title for the poem? Think of as many reasons as you can.

Developing a personal response

Activity 4

1 a What is your immediate response to the feelings expressed by the narrator?
b Do you think the narrator is aware that this is a likely response, even trying to provoke it?

2 The narrator's feelings are rarely expressed directly. Instead, they emerge through a series of metaphors. Why do you think this is?

3 a The mood of this poem has been described as: romantic humorous disturbing
Write down two other words that might describe its mood.
b Look at these key quotations from the poem:

'You move before me with all the unknowing ease of your age'

When you speak, shyness makes your words short, and your hesitancy touches my heart.'

'You are a choice meal,'

'I would leave nothing'

'who could wish to make away such innocence, such perfection?'

'using his life, sucking it out of him.'

'stay clear.'

'I'd let my tongue learn each taste and texture: the warm flesh juices and the eyes' salt; the mind's crisp freshness'

'your parasite, your predator'

How does each quotation contribute to the mood? Copy the table below, leaving space to write in each box, and then put the quotations in the relevant columns. Use the blank columns to add your own ideas from (a) above.

QUOTATIONS	MOOD				
	Romantic	Humorous	Disturbing	?	?

c What is the predominant mood of the poem?

Peer/Self-assessment

1 **Write two paragraphs responding to the task:**
How is the narrator's attitude towards a young person presented in 'Sweet 18'?

2 **Look at the grade descriptors on pages 148–155. What grade would you award your response?**

3 **What could you change or add to improve your response? Use the grade descriptors to identify the two things most likely to improve your grade.**

4 **Redraft your answer, trying to make those changes.**

5 **Look again at the grade descriptors. Have you improved your grade?**

Do Not Go Gentle Into That Good Night

by Dylan Thomas

First thoughts

Activity 1

1 Dylan Thomas wrote this poem for his father. What does it suggest to you about:
  a the writer **b** his father
  c their relationship now, when one is still young and the other is old?

Looking more closely

Activity 2

1 In stanza 1, Thomas refers to
  'that good night' 'close of day' 'the dying of the light'
  a What does each refer to?
  b What do all three have in common? Try to think of at least two different answers.

2 Thomas goes on to say that 'Old age should burn and rave'.
  a What does the word 'burn' suggests? How does it connect with the imagery of this stanza?
  b A number of meanings for the word 'rave' are listed on the left. Which meaning do you think Thomas is suggesting? Write two or three sentences explaining your answer.

3 Stanzas 2–5 explore how different people react to death.
  a Compare these reactions.
  b What effect do you think Thomas wants these stanzas to have on his father?

4 Stanza 2 is about 'wise men' whose words 'forked no lightning'.
  a What does this suggest about the words of wise men?
  b Does this failing alter their attitude to death?

5 Stanza 3 is about 'Good men ... crying' that their 'frail deeds might have danced', but didn't.
  a How does this image build on the earlier ones in the poem?
  b Does this failing alter their attitude to death?

6 Stanza 4 is about 'Wild men' who 'caught and sang the sun' but later realised they had 'grieved it on its way'.
  a How does this image build on the earlier ones in the poem?
  b Does this failing alter their attitude to death?

7 **a** What do the lives of these three different groups of men have in common?
  b How are they similar to the 'Grave men' in stanza 5? How are they different?

My learning objectives

- to explore the themes of the poem, including old age
- to develop my response to Thomas's poem
- to assess my work on Thomas's poem against the criteria in Assessment Objective 2 (page 134).

Rave:
- to speak excitedly, noisily
- to rant incoherently or insanely
- to speak or write with great enthusiasm.

GradeStudio

MAKE THE GRADE

Examiner tips

You can achieve a high grade if you:
- make detailed reference to the ideas, language and structure Thomas uses to convey the narrator's thoughts and to create the poem's mood
- use well-chosen quotations from the poem to support your points on theme, content, language and structure
- explore comparisons and links that you can make between this poem about old age and other texts with similar themes.

8 In the final stanza, Thomas describes his father 'on the sad height'. Where is his father?

9 At the end, Thomas asks his father for 'fierce tears' to 'Curse, bless' him. What does this suggest about their relationship?

Developing your ideas

Activity 3

1 a How has Thomas organised the references to light and darkness in the poem?
  b Why do you think he has done this?

2 Look at the images Thomas uses to explore the experience of being alive:
'forked no lightning' 'danced in a green bay' 'the sun in flight' 'blaze like meteors'
All use the metaphor of light.
  a How else are they linked?
  b What does this suggest?

3 The poem uses only two different rhymes, and repetition throughout.
  a Identify at least two examples of repetition, and comment on their effect.
  b How do you think the poem's rigid structure contributes to the mood and tone of the poem? Does it create a tone of:
  - rage
  - anguish
  - despair
  - anger
  - calm
  - sadness
  - resignation
  - something else?

Developing a personal response

Activity 4

Look at this range of different responses to the task:

How does Thomas explore youth and age, and life and death, in 'Do Not Go Gentle Into That Good Night'?

- Thomas begs his father to fight the inevitability of aging and death.
- Thomas explores different people's experiences of life and their reaction to old age and death.
- Thomas uses rhyme and repetition to build a mood of subdued anger, which grows throughout the poem.

Turn each of these responses into point-evidence-explanation paragraphs by:

- finding evidence for each
- adding a sentence or two explaining how and why your evidence supports them.

Peer/Self-assessment

1 Look at your answer to Activity 4 above, and at the grade descriptors on pages 148–155. What grade would you award your answer?

2 What could you change or add to improve your response? Use the grade descriptors to identify the two things most likely to improve your grade.

3 Redraft your answer, trying to make those changes.

4 Look again at the grade descriptors. Have you improved your grade?

My learning objectives

- to explore the themes of the poem, including youth and age
- to develop my response to Shakespeare's poem
- to assess my work on Shakespeare's poem against the criteria in Assessment Objective 2 (page 134).

GradeStudio

MAKE THE GRADE

Examiner tips

You can achieve a high grade if you:

- make detailed reference to the language and structure Shakespeare uses to convey the narrator's thoughts
- use well-chosen quotations from the poem to support your points on theme, content, language and structure
- explore comparisons and links that you can make between this poem about youth and age and other texts with similar themes.

Poem Glossary

Crabbèd: bad tempered, or hunched, stooping
Pleasance: pleasure
Care: worry
Sport: playful fun
Shepherd: often used as a symbol of youth in Elizabethan and other love poetry
Hie thee: come here
Stay'st: wait

Crabbed Age and Youth

by William Shakespeare

Activity 1

First thoughts

1 This is a poem of opposites. How many can you spot?

2 Look at the title of the poem.
  a How does it immediately establish the content and structure of the poem?
  b The narrator's opinion is also strongly suggested in the title. How?

Activity 2

Looking more closely

1 In the opening lines, the narrator states that
'Crabbed Age and Youth Cannot live together:'
What do you think may have prompted the poet to write this poem?

2 For much of the poem, the narrator compares age and youth. Make a list of all the ways in which they are described. You could record your answers in a table like the one below.

Youth	Age
full of pleasance like summer morn	full of care

3 The narrator compares youth to summer, and age to winter. Summer is described as 'brave' and winter as 'bare'. What do these two words suggest to you about summer and winter, and about youth and age?

4 In what ways is youth like summer and age like winter? Note down your responses in mind maps like the two opposite:

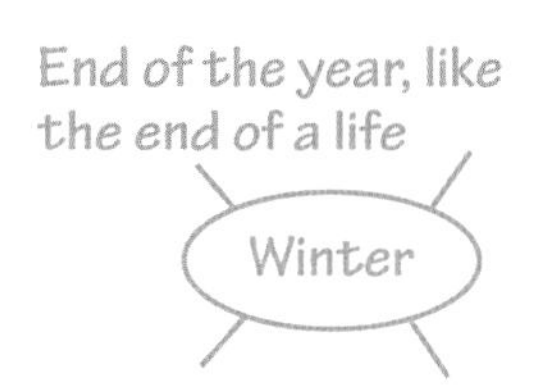

5 The narrator goes on to describe 'youth' as 'hot and bold' and 'wild' and 'age' as 'weak and cold' and 'tame'. How do these descriptions develop the idea of youth as a kind of summer, and age as a kind of winter?

6 Re-read the last two lines of the poem. After all the statements the narrator has made about youth and age, a decision seems to have been reached. What is it?

Developing your ideas

Activity 3

1 Throughout the poem, the narrator compares age and youth. What is the effect of this continual and developing contrast?

2 The narrator uses two dashes in the poem: one at the end of line 14, another at the end of line 18. How does this punctuation reflect the development of the narrator's thoughts?

3 Look at the structure of the poem as it builds towards the narrator's final decision. What tone does the poem's one stanza and short lines help to create?

Developing a personal response

Activity 4

1 Re-read the end of the poem. The narrator announces an intention to defy old age, and says that his/her love is young. Do you think this means that:
   - the person loved is young
   - his/her love for that person is young
   - both of these things
   - something else entirely?

   Support your answer with evidence from the poem.

2 How old do you think the narrator is?

3 What do you think is the narrator's gender?

4 Do you think the shepherd is a particular young person, or a symbol?

Peer/Self-assessment

1 Answer true or false to the following statements. I can find evidence for and comment on:
   - **a** the narrator's attitude to youth
   - **b** the narrator's attitude to age
   - **c** the narrator's use of imagery in the poem
   - **d** the structure of the poem and its effect
   - **e** different possible interpretations of the poem
   - **f** my response to the poem.

2 If you answered 'false' to any statements, compare your ideas with a partner's. Look again at the poem and your answers to the questions on these pages to help you.

3 What else can you say about this poem? Write a new set of true/false statements to assess a partner's understanding of 'Crabbed Age and Youth'.

4 **a** Write two paragraphs responding to the task: **How does Shakespeare present ideas on youth and age in 'Crabbed Age and Youth'?**
   b Look at the grade descriptors on pages 148–155. What grade would you award your response?

Porphyria's Lover

by Robert Browning

My learning objectives

- to explore the themes of the poem, including power and ambition
- to develop my response to Browning's poem
- to assess my work on Browning's poem against the criteria in Assessment Objective 2 (page 134).

GradeStudio

MAKE THE GRADE

Examiner tips

You can achieve a high grade if you:

- make detailed reference to the language and structure Browning uses to convey the narrator's thoughts
- use well-chosen quotations from the poem to support your points on theme, content, language and structure
- explore comparisons and links that you can make between this poem on power and ambition and texts with similar themes.

First thoughts

Activity 1

1 What is your first reaction to the poem's title? What questions might you like to ask about the poem?

2 There is much description of Porphyria, but little of her lover. Look for any information you can find about him. Why do you think Browning keeps this figure to a shadowy presence?

Looking more closely

Activity 2

1 What do we find out about Porphyria and her social situation? Can you find evidence for the following?
   a She is wealthy
   b She attends lavish parties
   c She is expected to marry someone from her own background
   d She is particularly beautiful

2 The poem begins with a depressing atmosphere. Look at the description in the first column below and match it to the appropriate quotation and meaning.

Atmosphere	Quotation	Meaning
A feeling of neglect and resentment	'The rain set early in to-night'	The trees are being described as being savaged by the violence of the wind
The narrator of the poem is desperately unhappy	'The sullen wind was soon awake'	The word 'heart' shows that he is suffering because of his feelings of love
A depressing feeling that even the weather has turned against him	'It tore the elm-tops down for spite'	It is miserable and wet and he feels trapped indoors. The weather matches his mood
A hint of revenge and destructive rage	'I listened with heart fit to break'	The weather is personified, and sounds unhappy and depressed

3 What drastic action does the narrator decide to take? Why do you think he decides to do this? Does the balance of power change?

4 The poem is a dramatic monologue – the narrator speaks directly to the reader – so we hear about the situation from only one point of view. What effect does this have? Look at the following words used to describe the narrator and decide which four best reflect your view of him. Find evidence from the text to support your ideas.

romantic	mistreated	selfish	loving	unhappy
blinded	desperate	ecstatic	unbalanced	calm
calculating	controlling	suicidal	controlled	self-righteous

Poem Glossary

Sullen: gloomy or sulky
Vex: trouble or torment
Grate: part of the fireplace where the fire usually burns
Endeavour: effort
Dissever: break away from
Tress: strand of hair
Utmost: greatest
Scorned: laughed at or looked down on

Developing your ideas

Activity 3

Look at this list of techniques that Browning uses to engage the reader, and match them to the quotations below. Then think about the effect they have on the reader.

- Personification of the weather
- Creation of a depressing atmosphere
- Repetition of key words
- Non-violent description of a violent death
- Use of exclamation marks
- The narrator attempting to convince the reader he has done the right thing

'mine, mine'

'The rain set early in to-night'

'So glad it has its utmost will'

'It tore the elm-tops down for spite'

'all her hair
In one long yellow string I wound'

'And yet God has not said a word!'

Developing a personal response

Activity 4

Browning shocks the reader with an unexpected ending.

1 What happens at the end?

2 Many people have found the last two lines disturbing. What is your reaction to them?

Peer/Self-assessment

MAKE THE GRADE

1 Read this paragraph, written in response to the task:
How does Browning explore the theme of power and ambition in 'Porphyria's Lover'?

2 Write a paragraph giving your own response to the task. Use the same structure as the paragraph on the right.

3 Annotate your paragraph using the same notes as the paragraph on the right. If you have forgotten to include anything in your paragraph, add it in.

4 Which criteria in Assessment Objective 2 on page 134 have you demonstrated in your paragraph?

Evidence used to support the point

A clear point

The narrator appears to have very little power in the start of the poem:
'When glided in Porphyria'.
The lover does not have any control. He has been passively and desperately waiting for his lover. She is described as 'gliding in', which suggests that she is completely in control and very calm. Browning appears to have some sympathy with the abandoned lover, because of the way he describes the weather and her arrival.

Close focus on the writer's word choice

How it reflects the poet's point of view

An explanation of the effect of the quotation

I Have Longed to Move Away

by Dylan Thomas

My learning objectives

- to understand the themes of the poem, including power and ambition
- to develop my response to Thomas's poem
- to assess my work on Thomas's poem against the criteria in Assessment Objective 2 (page 134).

Poem Glossary

Spent: used up or exhausted
Salutes: gestures of greeting, particularly associated with the military
Convention: established way of doing things

Activity 1

First thoughts

1 What does the title suggest the poem might be about? What might the narrator wish to move away from?

2 Read stanza 1 aloud. What sort of tone is most suitable? Experiment and decide whether it should be read in a threatening, angry, sinister, carefree, anxious or resigned way.

Activity 2

Looking more closely

1 Look at the things the narrator dislikes. Consider how they are described and what they might relate to, then copy and complete the following table.

Dislikes	Explanation and comment on language
'the hissing of the spent lie'	The word 'hissing' is unpleasant – it sounds like a snake, or something evil. The word is onomatopoeic. It suggests that he realises that something is an old lie and he wants to start afresh
'the old terrors' continual cry'	
'repetition of salutes'	
'ghosts in the air'	
'the thunder of calls and notes'	

2 Pick out all the imagery connected with war and the military. What do these suggest about the narrator's feelings?

Activity 3

Developing your ideas

1 In a letter about his early life in a small town in Wales, Thomas comments:

> *'Life passes the windows and I hate it more minute by minute. I see the rehearsed gestures, the correct smiles, the grey cells revolving around nothing under the godly bowlers'.*

(*The Collected Letters of Dylan Thomas*, edited by Paul Ferris, Weidenfeld & Nicolson, 2000.)

a What does he dislike about small-town living?

b Can you see any links between the behaviour described in his letter and that of people in the poem? Why might Thomas feel annoyed by such behaviour?

2 In stanza 2 Thomas gives some reasons for his failure to leave. What do you think the following lines mean?
'I have longed to move away but am afraid;
Some life, yet unspent, might explode
Out of the old lie burning on the ground'

3 The word 'lie' is used three times in the poem. Do you think this is significant? Is there any connection between the idea of lying and the narrator's failure to act on his own ambition to leave?

4 Students have made the following comments about the poem. Decide whether you agree or disagree with each. Find evidence from the poem to support your ideas.

Student A

'Although the narrator wants to spread his wings and break free from tradition, he is frightened of what the future might bring.'

Student B

'There is a great deal of anger and frustration in this poem. The narrator feels suffocated by the traditions and forced politeness of society.'

Student C

'This poem is about rebellion. The narrator would rather die than live a life governed by rules and conventions he does not care about.'

GradeStudio

Examiner tips

You can achieve a high grade if you:
- make detailed reference to the language and structure Thomas uses to convey the narrator's thoughts
- use well-chosen quotations from the poem to support your points on theme, content, language and structure
- explore comparisons and links you can make between this poem about power and ambition and other texts with similar themes.

Developing a personal response

Activity 4

1 How successful do you think the poet is in expressing conflict between the life he is living and the life he wants? Find a quotation to support your idea.

2 Look at the last two lines of the poem. What do you think of this as an ending? Do you think it ends on a positive note?

Peer/Self-assessment

1 Read this paragraph, written in response to the task:
How does Thomas present ambition in 'I Have Longed to Move Away'?

2 Write a paragraph giving your own response to the task. Use the same structure as the paragraph on the right.

3 Annotate your paragraph using the same notes as the paragraph on the right. If you have forgotten to include anything in your paragraph, add it in.

4 Which criteria in Assessment Objective 2 on page 134 have you demonstrated in your paragraph?

Evidence to support the point

A clear point

The narrator shows some fear about realising his ambition to leave his old life behind:
'Some life, yet unspent, might explode ... And, crackling into the air, leave me half-blind.'
The word 'explode', and the onomatopoeia in the word 'crackling', show the power still present in his old life. Both words are often associated with flames, and the suggestion that he might become 'half-blind' shows how it still has power to hurt him.

Here it reflects the poet's point of view

An explanation of the effect of the quotation

Leisure

by W. H. Davies

My learning objectives

- to explore the themes of the poem, including power and ambition
- to develop my response to Davies's poem
- to assess my work on Davies's poem against the criteria in Assessment Objective 2 (page 134).

GradeStudio

Examiner tips

You can achieve a high grade if you:

- make detailed reference to the language and structure Davies uses to convey the narrator's thoughts
- use well-chosen quotations from the poem to support your points on theme, content, language and structure
- explore comparisons and links you can make between this poem about power and ambition and other texts with similar themes.

Poem Glossary

Care: worry or concern
Boughs: branches of a tree
Enrich: enhance or improve

Activity 1

First thoughts

1 Think about your ideal day. What would it include? Where would you be? What time would you get up? How would it be different from a normal school day? Share your ideas with a partner.

2 Read the poem aloud. Try using different tones of voice to create a suitably relaxing and pleasant mood. Are there particular words that you should emphasise?

Activity 2

Looking more closely

1 What attitude do you think the narrator of this poem has towards his everyday life? What clues can you find to support your ideas?

2 What are the narrator's ambitions? How are they different from most people's?

3 The narrator mentions various pleasant activities that he feels he has no time for. List them, and discuss why you think he has selected them.

Activity 3

Developing your ideas

1 The poem is set out very simply, with two-line stanzas and some repetitive phrases. In pairs, consider why you think the poet has used such a simple form.

2 The poet uses various techniques to put his ideas across. In the following table, match the writer's technique, an example from the poem, and its intended effect.

Writer's technique	Example	Intended effect
Personification	'What is this life ...?'	Summarises the effect of beauty by making it seem like a living person
Rhetorical question	'No time to turn at Beauty's glance'	Reinforces the frantic pace of life and suggests the narrator is on a treadmill
Descriptions of nature	'No time to stand … No time to see'	Encourages the reader to question life and agree with the poet's viewpoint
Repetition	'And stare as long as sheep or cows'	Makes a contrast between the relaxing pace of nature and busy human lives

3 This poem considers the natural world at different times of day and night, and from different viewpoints. List these descriptions.

4 Select one line that you find the most persuasive in suggesting we should slow down and enjoy our surroundings more. Compare your choice with a partner's.

Activity 4

Developing a personal response

1 Do you think people rush about too much? This poem was written at the beginning of the twentieth century. Is life more or less stressful now than when the poem was written?

2 Some students have given their views on what they think this poem is about. For each one, say how far you agree, and find evidence from the poem to support your ideas.

Student A

'The poet appears to be suggesting that animals have a better life than we do because they aren't always hurrying about. It reminds us that we want too many material things and have too many ambitions. We should learn to stop sometimes and enjoy the moment.'

Student B

'I find this poem really relaxing to read. Even if you are busy, just hearing about all the natural wonders in the world makes it seem a better place. It seems to say: enjoy nature and make the most of each day.'

Student C

'This poem is unrealistic and overly sentimental. We can't be relaxed like the animals – we have bills to pay, work to do, exams to pass. That is the reality of life, if we want to be anyone or get anywhere. This poem shows a lack of ambition or hope in the narrator.'

Peer/Self-assessment

1 Answer true or false to the following statements.
I can find evidence for and comment on:
- a the narrator's love of the natural world
- b the narrator's feeling that life is too busy
- c the narrator's use of the different senses
- d how the structure of the poem reflects the idea that life can be too busy
- e my response to the poem.

2 If you answered 'false' to any statements, compare your ideas with a partner's.
Look again at the poem and your answers to the questions on these pages to help you.

3 a Write two paragraphs responding to the task:
How does Davies present modern life in 'Leisure'?

b Look at the grade descriptors on pages 148–155. What grade would you award your response?

My learning objectives

- to explore the themes of the poem, including power and ambition
- to develop my response to Duffy's poem
- to assess my work on Duffy's poem against the criteria in Assessment Objective 2 (page 134).

GradeStudio

Examiner tips

You can achieve a high grade if you:

- make detailed reference to the language and structure Duffy uses to convey the narrator's thoughts
- use well-chosen quotations from the poem to support your points on theme, content, language and structure
- explore comparisons and links you can make between this poem about power and ambition and other texts with similar themes.

Poem Glossary

Banged up inside: slang for 'locked up in prison'
Straight up: slang for 'I'm telling you the truth'

Human Interest

by Carol Ann Duffy

Activity 1

First thoughts

1 What has happened to a) the man, b) his girlfriend?

2 The poem has been written from the man's viewpoint – it is a dramatic monologue. Find evidence to show that we are hearing his story from his own particular viewpoint.

Activity 2

Looking more closely

1 The language in this poem has been deliberately selected to create an effect. Find examples of where the poet uses:
- slang
- physical description
- an image of an object.

Think about why each one has been used, and its effect on the reader. For example:

> The poet uses slang when the narrator describes his situation. 'Fifteen years minimum, banged up inside' gets across the fact that the narrator is serving a long prison sentence. The slang makes him sound tough and streetwise. The word 'banged' is also violent and makes the reader wonder what sort of crime he has done to get this long sentence.

2 Look carefully at stanza 1 where he describes his crime. What do you notice about the way he describes his actions?

3 Look again at the poem as a whole. Imagine you are interviewing this prisoner. There are some inconsistencies in what he is saying. You can ask him three questions to establish the truth of what happened. What will you ask?

Developing your ideas

Activity 3

1 The narrator does not mention his girlfriend's name. Why do you think this is? What effect would it have if he said her name, such as 'Kate', rather than calling her 'she'?

2 a The poem has been written as if it is one side of a conversation. It sounds as if the narrator is responding to a question. What do you think the question was?
  b List all the verbs (action words) used in the poem. What do you notice about them? Why do you think they have been used?
  c The poem has short sentences and strong statements. Find three examples of these. Why do you think Duffy chooses to write in this way? What effect does it have?

Developing a personal response

Activity 4

1 What impression do we get of the girlfriend? What are your thoughts about her? Look at the three comments below and decide which you agree with most. Support your ideas with quotations from the text.

Student A

'I think she is depicted as a cheating, deceitful woman. You can tell this by the words he uses. It is possible to have some sympathy for the man, as he was clearly being used.'

Student B

'We don't find out much about his girlfriend, but he sounds a violent and impatient man, so it would have been hard for her to leave him. The fact that the other man gave her 'a silver heart' suggests that she loved somebody else and he would have treated her better.'

Student C

'I think it is most interesting that we don't know her name. Her boyfriend kills her but can't even say her name. Instead he calls her 'My baby'. The word 'my' is used in a very possessive and jealous way. This shows he treated her like an object and killed her when she disobeyed.'

2 Why do you think the narrator killed his girlfriend? What was it about his personality, situation or attitude to life that made him unable to walk away from her?

Peer/Self-assessment

1 Write two paragraphs responding to the task:
How does Duffy present the abuse of power in 'Human Interest'?
2 Look at the grade descriptors on pages 148–155. What grade would you award your response?
3 What could you change or add to improve your response? Use the grade descriptors to identify the two things most likely to improve your grade.
4 Redraft your answer, trying to make those changes.
5 Look again at the grade descriptors. Have you improved your grade?

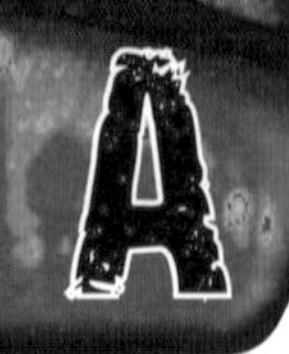

My learning objectives

- to explore the themes of the poem, including power and ambition
- to develop my response to Hughes's poem
- to assess my work on Hughes's poem against the criteria in Assessment Objective 2 (page 134).

GradeStudio

MAKE THE GRADE

Examiner tips

You can achieve a high grade if you:

- make detailed reference to the language and structure Hughes uses to convey the narrator's thoughts
- use well-chosen quotations from the poem to support your points on theme, content, language and structure
- explore comparisons and links you can make between this poem about power and ambition and other texts with similar themes.

Poem Glossary

Falsifying: deceptive, deliberately untrue
Buoyancy: supportiveness
Sophistry: clever but deceitful reasoning
Allotment: allocation, dealing out

Hawk Roosting

by Ted Hughes

Activity 1

First thoughts

1 This poem is about a hawk. In pairs, jot down ideas connected to hawks under the following topics: skills, looks, human attitudes towards them, how they have been used in history.

2 Read the poem aloud. It is a dramatic monologue (one person speaking), written from the hawk's perspective. Try reading it in a range of different tones to establish the right 'voice' for this character.

Activity 2

Looking more closely

1 Why do you think Hughes writes the poem from the bird's viewpoint?

2 What impression do you get of the hawk? Look at the words below and pick out two that you think are particularly appropriate. Support your ideas with evidence from the text.

arrogant	happy	dignified	violent	controlled
excited	kind	resourceful	serene	thoughtful
cruel	remorseful	godlike	nervous	self-indulgent
proud	respectful	majestic	destructive	hard-working

3 What happens in the poem? Describe the action of the poem in a sentence. Why do you think Hughes chooses this moment to describe the hawk?

Activity 3

Developing your ideas

1 Hughes uses a range of techniques to bring his view of the hawk to life. Look at the range of techniques listed below, find an example from the poem for each, and discuss its effect. The first one has been done for you.

Poet's technique	Example	Effect created
Repetition	'my hooked head and hooked feet'	The word 'hooked' gives the reader a clear visual impression of the bird's feet and head. It also suggests a certain power and perhaps danger, as hooks are sharp and can be painful. This is reinforced through the repetition.
Use of an exclamation mark		
Violent vocabulary		
Very short sentences		

2 For each stanza, note down what the hawk is doing. Look carefully at the verbs (words that describe actions) that are connected with the hawk. What do you notice about them?

3 Hughes describes the hawk and its actions in great detail. What attitude do you think he has towards the hawk?

4 Discuss the following lines. Think about whether the poet admires, respects or dislikes the hawk in each one. Make sure you can give clear reasons for your answer.

'It took the whole of Creation
To produce my foot'

'I am going to keep things like this'

'No arguments assert my right'

'I kill where I please because it is all mine'

Activity 4

Developing a personal response

1 How do you respond to the description of the hawk? For example, do you find its power and ambition inspiring or horrifying?

2 In pairs, write a five-minute speech arguing either that a) the hawk is described by Hughes with respect as a skilful killing machine, or b) Hughes describes the hawk as a cold-blooded murderer and finds its violence unpleasant.

3 Some readers have suggested that the poem is not just about a hawk, but can be related to wider ideas of power and ambition in people and society. What do you think? Can the themes of the poem be related to society, or is it just about a powerful force of nature? If the poem is referring to a person, what type of person is it?

4 If you were asked to describe this poem and its effect on you in ten words, what would you say? In your description, select the line from the poem that has the biggest impact on you.

Peer/Self-assessment

MAKE THE GRADE

1 Answer true or false to the following statements.
I can find evidence for and comment on:

a the hawk's power
b the hawk's feeling of control and supremacy
c the hawk's enjoyment of its life
d how the poet seems to admire the hawk
e how the poem seems to celebrate the bird's life
f how the poem draws attention to frightening or troubling aspects of the hawk
g my response to the poem.

2 If you answered 'false' to any statements, compare your ideas with a partner's. Look again at the poem and your answers to the questions on these pages to help you.

3 a Write two paragraphs responding to the task:
How does Hughes present power and ambition in 'Hawk Roosting'?

b Look at the grade descriptors on pages 148–155. What grade would you award your response?

My Last Duchess

by Robert Browning

My learning objectives

- to explore the themes of the poem, including power and ambition
- to develop my response to Browning's poem
- to assess my work on Browning's poem against the criteria in Assessment Objective 2 (page 134).

GradeStudio

MAKE THE GRADE MAKE THE GRADE

Examiner tips

You can achieve a high grade if you:

- make detailed reference to the language and structure Browning uses to convey the narrator's thoughts
- use well-chosen quotations from the poem to support your points on theme, content, language and structure
- explore comparisons and links you can make between this poem about power and ambition and other texts with similar themes.

Poem Glossary

Frà Pandolf: name of (imaginary) famous painter
Countenance: face
Durst: dare
Mantle: woman's cape
Courtesy: politeness
Officious: giving unwanted service
Forsooth: certainly
Munificence: generosity
Pretence: claim
Dowry: property a wife brings to her husband on marrying
Avowed: stated, affirmed
Neptune: Roman god of the sea

First thoughts

Activity 1

1 Look at the first two lines of the poem:
'That's my last Duchess painted on the wall,
Looking as if she were alive.'
With a partner, think of three things that you think may have happened.

2 What two questions would you like to ask the Duke?

Looking more closely

Activity 2

1 The Duke is the only speaker, which makes this a dramatic monologue. He speaks in a measured and even graceful way, but the things he suggests are in fact quite startling. What is the effect of this?

2 Look at his description of the Duchess. Which of the following statements can you find evidence for in the poem?
- She blushed easily
- She loved her husband
- She treated all people equally
- She was a flirt
- She was polite
- She was ungrateful to the Duke

3 The Duke gives away his attitude towards his wife with each comment he makes. Match up the words that describe his attitude with the appropriate quotation and meaning in the table below.

Duke's attitude	Quotation	Meaning
Proud	'since none puts by / The curtain I have drawn for you, but I'	I have supreme control and my orders are carried out. I do not need to undertake any unpleasant task – I have servants to do that for me
Controlling	'That's my last Duchess painted on the wall'	It is beneath me to explain myself or ask others to change their ways. They should already know how to behave
Disdainful	'I gave commands; / Then all smiles stopped together.'	I am the owner of the portrait and the person who controls when it is viewed.
Refuses to explain himself or compromise	'She thanked men,— good!'	It is appropriate to be polite, but certainly not to treat all people equally
Authoritarian and rather frightening	'E'en then would be some stooping; and I choose / Never to stoop.'	She belongs to me, and her fate could be considered a warning to other women who don't give me total respect

Developing your ideas

Activity 3

1. The poem builds up a picture of the Duchess's life with the Duke. What information can you find on what life was like for her?
2. What do we learn about the Duke and his current situation? Think about who is visiting him and why.

Developing a personal response

Activity 4

Students have written the following notes on their response to the poem. Select two points that you agree with and two you disagree with. For each, find evidence from the poem to support your view.

Student A

'The Duke is presented as an unsympathetic tyrant.'

Student B

'The Duke's story is really a warning and a message to his next Duchess.'

Student C

'Browning appears to see the Duke as an obsessive and irrational character.'

Student D

'We feel sorry for the Duke.'

Student E

'We feel that the Duchess was probably a flirt.'

Student F

'The Duchess is presented as an innocent victim of a jealous man.'

Peer/Self-assessment

MAKE THE GRADE

1. Read this paragraph, written in response to the task:
   How does Browning present power and ambition in 'My Last Duchess'?
2. Write a paragraph giving your own response to the task. Use the same structure as the paragraph on the right.
3. Annotate your paragraph using the same notes as the paragraph on the right. If you have forgotten to include anything in your paragraph, add it in.
4. Which criteria in Assessment Objective 2 on page 134 have you demonstrated in your paragraph?

Evidence to support the point

A clear point

The narrator, the Duke, has a great deal of self-confidence:
'since none puts by
The curtain I have drawn for you, but I'
The language here illustrates the Duke's power and control. Throughout the poem he repeatedly uses 'I'. This suggests his self-obsession and his power. Browning is using the voice of a controlling narrator to show how completely he ruled over his wife – even to the extent of managing who could see her portrait.

An explanation of the effect of the quotation

How it reflects the poet's point of view

Close focus on the writer's choice of language

My learning objectives

- to explore the themes of the poem, including power and ambition
- to develop my response to Shelley's poem
- to assess my work on Shelley's poem against the criteria in Assessment Objective 2 (page 134).

GradeStudio

MAKE THE GRADE MAKE THE GRADE

Examiner tips

You can achieve a high grade if you:

- make detailed reference to the language and structure Shelley uses to convey the message of the poem
- use well-chosen quotations from the poem to support your points on theme, content, language and structure
- explore comparisons and links you can make between this poem about power and ambition and other texts with similar themes.

Ozymandias

by Percy Bysshe Shelley

Activity 1

First thoughts

The poem describes a half-ruined statue of a king found in a desert. Read it aloud, trying different tones of voice to create a suitable mood. Are there particular words that you think should be emphasised?

Activity 2

Looking more closely

1 The narrator retells a story he has been told. We also hear the voice of the dead king Ozymandias. What can you tell about these different voices? Why do you think Shelley decided to relate this poem as a traveller's tale?

2 What are your first impressions of Ozymandias as a ruler? Choose some of the words below. Support your ideas with quotations from the text.

fierce	uncaring	concerned	cold-hearted	brave
proud	disdainful	spiteful	tyrannical	intelligent
loyal	deceitful	frightening	egotistical	remorseful
confused	regal	dictatorial	sympathetic	
supportive	vain	heartless		

Activity 3

Developing your ideas

1 This poem is highly descriptive. Look at how Shelley describes the statue, then copy and complete the table below.

Example	What this means	Why Shelley chooses these words
'Two vast and trunkless legs of stone'	There are only two enormous legs – the body of the statue is gone	'Vast' suggests it was once a huge statue. It also suggests power. We wonder what the rest of it might have been like
'a shattered visage lies'		
'whose frown, / And wrinkled lip, and sneer of cold command'		
'My name is Ozymandias, king of kings'		
'Round the decay / Of that colossal wreck'		

2 What evidence is there that Ozymandias achieved great things in his life?

> **Poem Glossary**
>
> **Visage**: face
> **Sculptor**: person who carves objects from stone
> **Pedestal**: base for a statue
> **Colossal**: gigantic
> **Wreck**: ruin

Activity 4

Developing a personal response

1 Find the lines that refer to the sculptor who made the statue. Which of the comments below best fit the poet's view of the sculptor? Put the comments in order, starting with the one you agree with most. Support your ideas with quotations.
- The sculptor was trying to flatter Ozymandias by making such a statue.
- The sculptor did not make a good job of the statue because it is a ruin.
- The sculptor was almost mocking the arrogance of Ozymandias.
- The sculptor had great skill in making a piece of stone come to life.

2 People have different ideas about what this poem means. Decide which of the comments below you agree with, and find evidence from the poem to support your ideas.

Student A

'This poem shows that human power is limited. Even the most powerful rulers eventually are reduced to rubble in the desert.'

Student B

'This poem is all about the power of art and poetry. Although Ozymandias and the sculptor are long dead, the power of art lives on in the remains of the statue and in Shelley's poetry.'

Student C

'This poem is more about the power of nature and time than human power. The last line is the most important as it shows that eventually all that is left is the vast emptiness of the desert and eternity.'

Student D

'This poem is a reminder that people crave power like Ozymandias. They want to be in control, but all power is only temporary and the sculptor is left with the final word.'

Peer/Self-assessment

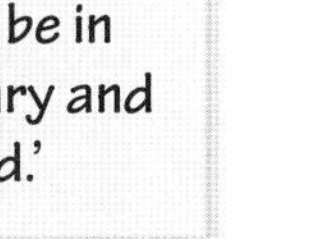

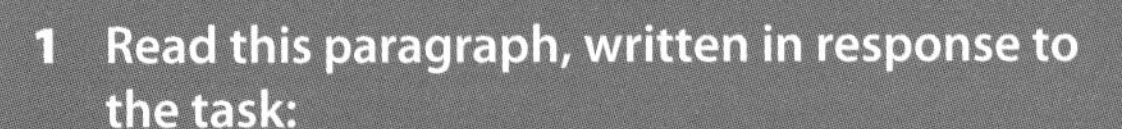

1 Read this paragraph, written in response to the task:

How does Shelley present power and ambition in 'Ozymandias'?

2 Write a paragraph giving your own response to the task. Use the same structure as the paragraph on the right.

3 Annotate your paragraph using the same notes as the paragraph on the right. If you have forgotten to include anything in your paragraph, add it in.

4 Which criteria in Assessment Objective 2 on page 134 have you demonstrated in your paragraph?

Evidence to support the point

A clear point

Shelley presents power and ambition in a strong, forceful way:
'whose frown,
And wrinkled lip, and sneer of cold command'
The 'sneer' suggests that Ozymandias is contemptuous and regal. He is seen as all-powerful and almost frightening, emphasised by the fact he 'frowns' as if with displeasure. However, Shelley undermines his power and ambition by ultimately representing him as just pieces of a broken statue in a vast desert.

An explanation of the effect of the quotation

How it reflects the poet's point of view

Close focus on the writer's choice of language

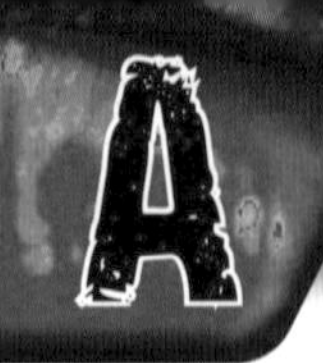

The Interrogation

by Edwin Muir

My learning objectives

- to understand the themes of the poem, including power
- to develop my response to Muir's poem
- to assess my work on Muir's poem against the criteria in Assessment Objective 2 (page 134).

GradeStudio

Examiner tips

You can achieve a high grade if you:

- make detailed reference to the language and structure Muir uses to convey the narrator's thoughts
- use well-chosen quotations from the poem to support your points on theme, content, language and structure
- explore comparisons and links you can make between this poem about power and other texts with similar themes.

Poem Glossary

Surly: grumpy
Indifferent: uninterested
Interrogation: formal, systematic questioning
Endurance: tolerance of suffering

First thoughts

Activity 1

1 Make a mind map of all the connections you can think of for the word 'interrogation'.

2 The opening line is unusual:
'We could have crossed the road but hesitated.'
What three questions would you like to ask about what is happening in this opening?

3 What can you find out about the people who could have crossed the road? Make a list of what you suspect about them, giving evidence from the poem.

Looking more closely

Activity 2

1 Re-read the first four lines of the poem. They describe the patrol and the way the people are stopped.
   a How does the poet describe the patrol?
   b How does the poet make the moment the people are stopped a tense one?

2 As the poem progresses, so does the interrogation. Find two words or lines that show how stressful the situation is for the people being interrogated.

3 Find three things that interest you about the following lines, and discuss them with a partner:
'The careless lovers in pairs go by,
Hand linked in hand, wandering another star'

4 The poem ends ambiguously – the reader is unsure what happens next:
'We are on the very edge,
Endurance almost done,
And still the interrogation is going on.'
Why do you think Muir ends the poem in this way?

Developing your ideas

Activity 3

1 Students have made the following comments on the poem. Decide whether you disagree or agree with each comment, and find evidence in the poem to support your opinion.

Student A

'This poem shows the power and control of those in authority. The patrol are the most frightening part of the poem.'

Student B

'This poem shows a contrast between weak and strong people. The people being interrogated do not act quickly enough and are caught because of this.'

Student C

'Muir shows a great deal of sympathy for the people being questioned. We can see this in the way he portrays their fear.'

Student D

'The setting of the poem by a road, near others who are obviously free, makes the situation even more threatening.'

Student E

'The poem is really about the fact that some groups of people are powerless to avoid their situation.'

2 The poem is structured in a particular way, and uses various poetic devices. In pairs, discuss the following choices Muir has made.

Technique	Effect on the reader	Why has it been written like this?
Uses the inclusive 'we'	Reader feels sympathy for the group; also feels involved	The use of the pronoun 'we' adds interest as well as involving the reader, as it is unclear who the people in the group are
The group are described as very passive; they don't act – they wait		
The poet uses full stops at some key moments		
The poet uses words that contrast with the tense situation, such as 'careless' and 'wandering'		
The whole poem is rather like an interrogation, raising various questions		

Activity 4

Developing a personal response

1 How successful do you think Muir is in presenting the theme of power in this poem?

2 If you had to explain what this poem was about in a couple of sentences, what would you say? Which line of the poem do you think best reflects the theme?

Peer/Self-assessment

1 Write two paragraphs responding to the task:
How does Muir show the abuse of power in 'The Interrogation'?

2 Look at the grade descriptors on pages 148–155. What grade would you award your response?

3 What could you change or add to improve your response? Use the grade descriptors to identify the two things most likely to improve your grade.

4 Redraft your answer, trying to make those changes.

5 Look again at the grade descriptors. Have you improved your grade?

They Did Not Expect This

by Vernon Scannell

My learning objectives

- to explore the themes of the poem, including male/female relationships
- to develop my response to Scannell's poem
- to assess my work on Scannell's poem against the criteria in Assessment Objective 2 (page 134).

GradeStudio

Examiner tips

You can achieve a high grade if you:

- make detailed reference to the language and structure Scannell uses to convey the narrator's thoughts
- use well-chosen quotations from the poem to support your points on theme, content, language and structure
- explore comparisons and links you can make between this poem about men and women and other texts with similar themes.

First thoughts

Activity 1

1 Look at the first sentence in the poem:
'They did not expect this.'
With a partner, think about the following:
- How effective is it as an opening?
- What sort of mood does it establish?
- How might this relate to the theme of male/female relationships?

2 Read the poem aloud. Try using different tones of voice to create a mood that you think is suitable. What sort of atmosphere do you think the poet wants to create?

Looking more closely

Activity 2

1 Working on your own, create a chart like the one below to jot down your first impressions. Consider what you think each stanza might be about. Try to write two ideas about each, and find evidence to support them. Finally, think of some questions you would like to ask about each stanza. Use the ideas below as a starting point.

Aspects of the poem	Evidence	My questions
Stanza 1: The people described seem to be fairly young	'And wearing only the beauty of youth's season'	Are they being described as a romantic couple? Is the poet suggesting youth is short-lived?
Stanza 1: Seems to suggest that the people got easily lost		
Stanza 2:	'Then the rain began and there was no shelter anywhere'	
Stanza 2:	'and the rows of houses stern as soldiers.'	

2 Share your chart with a partner and think about the questions you both posed. Working together, can you answer any of them?

3 Now prepare a final list of questions you would like to ask. For example: 'Why do the couple learn to believe in ghosts? Are these real ghosts?'

Poem Glossary

Endearing: expressing love
Seal: large marine animal
Mantelpiece: decorative shelf over a fireplace
Looking in the bottoms of teacups: fortune telling from tea leaves

Activity 3

Developing your ideas

1 Scannell once said that 'the business of poetry is to harmonise the sadness of the universe'. This poem could be seen as sad or depressing. Look at each stanza and add your ideas to the mind map:

Sad or depressing images

- Idea of getting lost and confused (stanza 1)
- 'nagged / By a small wind' sounds uncomfortable and unpleasant; 'nagging' suggests unhappy relationship and constant criticism
- 'their hope stuffed' sounds like a dead animal; 'hope' is such a cheerful word, but it seems to have died

2 Look carefully at the tenses the poet uses. Why do you think most of the poem is written in the past tense, and the last stanza in the present tense?

3 The poet uses the phrase 'They did not expect this' twice, and it is the poem's title. Why do you think he makes this choice? Why does he position it at the start and end of the poem? Is it the best title for the poem?

Activity 4

Developing a personal response

1 How do you respond to the situation in the poem? Do you think it gives a truthful picture of many long-term male/female relationships? Support your answer with ideas from the text.

2 We are not given much physical description of the couple. Look at what is included and what it tells you. Why do you think the poet largely concentrates on describing their surroundings?

3 If you were asked to describe this poem and its effect on you in ten words, what would you say? Can you summarise the plot quickly? What effect does it have on you? Is this what the writer intends?

Peer/Self-assessment

1 Answer true or false to the following statements.
I can find evidence for and comment on:
- a the lack of communication between the couple
- b the feeling of sadness in the poem
- c the way the weather and surroundings create a sombre mood
- d how the poet seems to pity the couple
- e how the poem seems to suggest that life and love are disappointing
- f my response to the poem.

2 If you answered 'false' to any statements, compare your ideas with a partner's.
Look again at the poem and your answers to the questions on these pages to help you.

3 a Write two paragraphs responding to the task:
How does Scannell present male/female relationships in 'They Did Not Expect This'?
b Look again at the grade descriptors on pages 148–155. What grade would you award your response?

My learning objectives

- to explore the themes of the poem, including male/female relationships
- to develop my response to MacNeice's poem
- to assess my work on MacNeice's poem against the criteria in Assessment Objective 2 (page 134).

GradeStudio

Examiner tips

You can achieve a high grade if you:

- make detailed reference to the language and structure MacNeice uses to convey the narrator's thoughts
- use well-chosen quotations from the poem to support your points on theme, content, language and structure
- explore comparisons and links you can make between this poem about men and women and other texts with similar themes.

Poem Glossary

Limpid: clear or transparent
Inverted: turned inwards or upside down
Poise: composure or balance
Brazen: (literally) made of brass; (metaphorically) impudent, rude
Calyx: the outer part of a flower, or a cuplike structure
Waltz: a dance for couples
Verify: confirm the truth or accuracy of something

Meeting Point

by Louis MacNeice

Activity 1

First thoughts

1 This poem is about when time appears to stand still because you are so wrapped up in something or someone. Think about the last time this happened to you. What were you doing? Why did time seem to stop?

2 There are several clues in stanza 1 that time has stopped because of the couple's interest in each other. Find as many of these as you can, and discuss them with a partner.

Activity 2

Looking more closely

1 Re-read the first three stanzas. It describes the surroundings the couple are in.
   a What information can you find about the setting of this poem?
   b Why do you think the poet might have chosen to set it in such a place?

2 In stanza 4 the couple seem to retreat even further into their own world. How does the poet achieve this effect?

3 Discuss the following lines with a partner:
   'the clock
   Forgot them and the radio waltz
   Came out like water from a rock'
   Write down two things that interest you about this description.

4 Stanza 6 describes the woman's actions:
   'Her fingers flicked away the ash
   That bloomed again in tropic trees:
   Not caring if the markets crash
   When they had forests such as these'
   a How do you think the woman feels here?
   b Choose one word that shows her emotions. Explain in a sentence why you think it has been used.

Activity 3

Developing your ideas

1 Look carefully at the poem's structure and language techniques. The following features have been used. For each one, think about why the poet has used it, and find an example to demonstrate this. The first has been done for you.
   - Personification (giving human characteristics to objects or ideas):

'the clock / Forgot them'	This makes it seem as if the couple are so wrapped up in each other that even the clock leaves them alone. It suggests that time stands still for them.

- The first and last lines of each stanza are the same.
- Sound effects such as alliteration are used.
- An extended image of a desert scene is used.

2 The narrator appears to make a judgement about the fact that time has stopped for the couple. What view does he express?

Developing a personal response

Activity 4

1 How would you describe the overall mood or atmosphere of the poem? Select two adjectives from the list below. For each, explain your reasons in a sentence and find at least one quotation to support your idea.

happy	jubilant	ecstatic	relaxed	mournful	thoughtful
romantic	mysterious	joyful	secretive	solemn	nostalgic
oppressive	loving	hopeful	cheerful	dull	
strained	exotic	euphoric	magical		

2 a We don't find out a great deal about the couple. Instead, it is as if we see them in a snapshot. But what can you tell about the relationship? Do you think they have recently met? Or are they long married? Do they seem to be meeting in secret? Discuss your ideas with a partner, and find evidence from the poem to support your views.

b Imagine you could ask the poet three questions to help you develop your ideas further. What might you ask?

3 If you were asked to describe this poem and its effect on you in ten words, what would you say? Can you summarise the poem quickly? What attitude does it show towards male/female relationships?

Peer/Self-assessment

1 Answer true or false to the following statements.
I can find evidence for and comment on:
- a the way the poet makes time appear to stop
- b how the setting becomes almost magical
- c the way the poet uses ordinary objects to create a timeless atmosphere
- d how the poet seems to rejoice in the couple's love
- e my response to the poem.

2 If you answered 'false' to any statements, compare your ideas with a partner's.
Look again at the poem and your answers to the questions on these pages to help you.

3 a Write two paragraphs responding to the task:
How does MacNeice present male/female relationships in 'Meeting Point'?

b Look again at the grade descriptors on pages 148–155. What grade would you award your response?

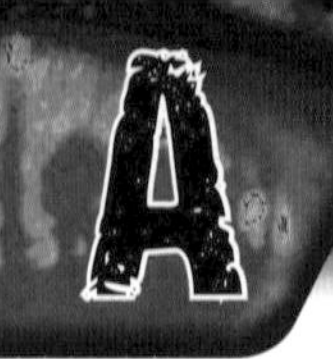

My learning objectives

- to explore the themes of the poem, including male/female relationships
- to develop my response to Larkin's poem
- to assess my work on Larkin's poem against the criteria in Assessment Objective 2 (page 134).

GradeStudio

Examiner tips

You can achieve a high grade if you:

- make detailed reference to the language and structure Larkin uses to convey the narrator's thoughts
- use well-chosen quotations from the poem to support your points on theme, content, language and structure
- explore comparisons and links you can make between this poem about men and women and other texts with similar themes.

Poem Glossary

Skilled trades: manual jobs that need skills, such as those done by electricians and plumbers
Courting-places: parts of the park where lovers meet and sit

Afternoons

by Philip Larkin

Activity 1

First thoughts

1 Look at the following descriptions. Then select two words from the list below that you think most relate to each situation. Compare your answer with a partner's and discuss the reasons for your choices.
- A teenage girl, in her first serious love affair, on a Saturday afternoon.
- A mother of two small children in her late twenties, on a Wednesday morning.

relaxed	frantic	exhilarated	happy	busy	curious
joyful	hopeful	delighted	frustrated	calm	excited
bored	worried	unhappy	thoughtful	miserable	careful
elated	anxious	desperate	stressed	serious	nervous

2 Larkin's poem is very descriptive and paints a clear picture of what can be seen. If you were asked to illustrate what was happening in each of the three stanzas, what would you include? For each, draw a quick sketch or write a detailed sentence explaining what it should show.

Activity 2

Looking more closely

1 This poem considers the situation of some women who are taking their small children to play at the recreation ground. Look at how the setting is described. Find examples from the poem to show that:
- **a** it is a newly developed area
- **b** the seasons are changing
- **c** the children are enjoying being at the recreation ground
- **d** the women's lives are full of domestic chores.

2 How do you think these women feel about their lives? Divide your page in half and list all the positive aspects you can find in the poem on one side, and all the negative or boring aspects on the other.

Negative aspects	Meaning	Positive aspects	Meaning
'An estateful of washing'	Their lives seem identical, since they live in similar 'estate' houses with no individuality. The idea of an 'estateful of washing' makes it sound a hard and tedious life		

3 Overall, did you find the presentation of the women's lives to be more positive or negative? Write three sentences explaining your thoughts, and use quotations to support your ideas.

4 What do you think is meant by the phrase 'Summer is fading'? Mind map any ideas you have about how this relates to the poem as a whole.

Activity 3

Developing your ideas

Look at the following lines and discuss them in pairs. What do you think they mean? The first one has been annotated with some ideas.

'In the hollows of afternoons
Young mothers assemble'

'At swing and sandpit
Setting free their children.'

'Before them, the wind
Is ruining their courting-places'

'Their beauty has thickened.
Something is pushing them
To the side of their own lives.'

'In the hollows of afternoons
Young mothers assemble'

- hollows: Suggests quite a sad mood. Are the afternoons (and their lives) empty, as they have been 'hollowed' out? Might also refer to areas where girls used to go with boyfriends in happier summers.
- afternoons: Could be the literal afternoon but might suggest (like the image of summer) these women are getting older, in the afternoons of their lives.
- Young: Suggests that they have quite recently been carefree and youthful
- assemble: Suggests that the park is no longer fun. A semi-formal group of mothers are there to watch over their children.

Activity 4

Developing a personal response

1 Look carefully at stanza 2. What is suggested about the everyday lives and hopes of these women and their husbands?

2 Time and its passing are very important in this poem. In pairs, consider the reasons why Larkin does the following:
   a sets the poem at the end of summer
   b makes the women *young* mothers
   c describes lovers as being still 'in school'
   d describes the women's beauty as 'thickened'
   e ends the poem in the way that he does.

Peer/Self-assessment

MAKE THE GRADE

1 Write two paragraphs responding to the task:
   How are male/female relationships presented in 'Afternoons' by Philip Larkin?
2 Look at the grade descriptors on pages 148–155. What grade would you award your response?
3 What could you change or add to improve your response? Use the grade descriptors to identify the two things most likely to improve your grade.
4 Redraft your answer, trying to make those changes.
5 Look again at the grade descriptors. Have you improved your grade?

Havisham

by Carol Ann Duffy

My learning objectives

- to explore the themes of the poem, including male/female relationships
- to develop my response to Duffy's poem
- to assess my work on Duffy's poem against the criteria in Assessment Objective 2 (page 134).

GradeStudio

Examiner tips

You can achieve a high grade if you:

- make detailed reference to the language and structure Duffy uses to convey the narrator's thoughts
- use well-chosen quotations from the poem to support your points on theme, content, language and structure
- explore comparisons and links you can make between this poem about men and women and other texts with similar themes.

First thoughts

Activity 1

1 Look at the first half-line:
'Beloved sweetheart bastard.'
With a partner, discuss what you think a poem starting like this will be about.

2 This poem is spoken by a narrator. What two things do you think have happened to her? What questions might you like to ask the speaker?

Looking more closely

Activity 2

1 This poem is narrated by Miss Havisham, a character in Charles Dickens's novel *Great Expectations*, who is jilted on her wedding day and never recovers. She is still wearing her wedding dress as she grows older and becomes more mentally unbalanced.

Why do you think Duffy calls her poem 'Havisham' rather than 'Miss Havisham'?

2 There are many clues that the narrator has a twisted and unnatural view of the world. Some are listed below; make notes to show what they suggest. The first has been done for you.

'I've dark green pebbles for eyes'

'ropes on the back of my hands I could strangle with.'

'Whole days / in bed
cawing Nooooo at the wall'

'I stink and remember.'

'Dark' suggests death and decay

Suggests small, cold, hard

'I've dark green pebbles for eyes'

The colour associated with jealousy. Perhaps showing she cannot forgive or move on?

Developing your ideas

Activity 3

1 Many of the verbs (action words) in the poem suggest actions that are violent or hurtful. Make a note of the actions and place them on a continuum line like the one below, according to how violent they are. Give a reason for your placement of each.

Peaceful ⟷ Violent

For example, 'stink' could be placed to the right of midway, because it does not suggest violence but is unpleasant and invasive.

2 This poem is about a male/female relationship – yet the man is not present. What can you discover about the missing man and the narrator's attitude towards him? Copy and complete the chart below.

Clue from the text	What it suggests	Comment on the language
'Give me a male corpse for a long slow honeymoon.'	She still desires him because she wants a 'honeymoon', but wishes for his death even more strongly.	'Give' seems demanding. Horrible contrast between 'honeymoon' and 'male corpse'
'the lost body over me'		
'Beloved sweetheart bastard'		
'my fluent tongue in its mouth in its ear'		

Activity 4

Developing a personal response

Students have written the following notes on their responses to the poem. Select one you agree with and one you disagree with. For each, find evidence from the poem to support your view.

Poem Glossary

Spinster: unmarried woman
Cawing: crying sound a crow makes
Slewed: tilted, distorted
Puce: deep purplish pink colour

Student A

'Havisham is depicted as so disturbed and with such violent fantasies that we don't feel sympathy for her, only disgust.'

Student B

'This poem shows how some people are unable to move on after a broken relationship and their bitterness ends up destroying them.'

Student C

'The reader feels immense sympathy for Havisham; she is presented as a figure needing love.'

Student D

'This is one of the most violent poems I have come across. It seems less about relationships and more about hate.'

Peer/Self-assessment

MAKE THE GRADE

1 Read this paragraph, written in response to the task:
How does Duffy present male/female relationships in 'Havisham'?
2 Write a paragraph giving your own response to the task. Use the same structure as the paragraph on the right.
3 Annotate your paragraph using the same notes as the paragraph on the right. If you have forgotten to include anything in your paragraph, add it in.
4 Which criteria in Assessment Objective 2 on page 134 have you demonstrated in your paragraph?

Evidence to support the point

A clear point

The narrator of the poem seems half-crazed, and sustained by violent fantasy:
'Puce curses that are sounds not words.'
The language here shows her loss of control. The word 'curses' shows malevolence and the colour 'Puce' suggests a horrible, angry, frightening colour, like her mood. She is so angry that she is unable to utter proper words – like an animal, she just makes a noise.

An explanation of the effect of the quotation

How language reflects the poet's point of view

Close focus on the writer's choice of language

To the Virgins, To Make Much of Time

by Robert Herrick

My learning objectives

- to explore the themes of the poem, including male/female relationships
- to develop my response to Herrick's poem
- to assess my work on Herrick's poem against the criteria in Assessment Objective 2 (page 134).

GradeStudio

Examiner tips

You can achieve a high grade if you:

- make detailed reference to the language and structure Herrick uses to convey the poet's message
- use well-chosen quotations from the poem to support your points on theme, content, language and structure
- explore comparisons and links you can make between this poem about men and women and other texts with similar themes.

Poem Glossary

Spent: used up and exhausted
Coy: pretending to be shy
Prime: height of physical perfection and strength
Tarry: delay or wait

Activity 1

First thoughts

1 Experiment with reading the poem aloud in different ways, capturing different moods. Try changing the pace and emphasis until you have a reading you are pleased with.

2 This poem is often used as a reading at weddings. Find three things that you think make it suitable for a wedding service. How do you feel about using it in this way?

Activity 2

Looking more closely

1 The reader of this poem is encouraged to 'seize the moment' and enjoy today. Look for different ways in which the poet encourages this attitude. For example, the image of 'rosebuds' suggests something fresh and beautiful that will not last long.

2 Who do you think is the speaker of the poem? Is it the poet, or is he adopting another 'voice'?

3 People have different reactions to this poem. How does it make you feel? Look at the adjectives in the list below and select one or two that you agree with. Then use them in a sentence. For example: 'This poem makes me feel happy and relieved because I'm young, and I still have the opportunity to "seize the day"'.

anxious	guilty	relieved	excited	disappointed	thoughtful
carefree	concerned	hopeful	unhappy	nervous	annoyed
surprised	happy	regretful	amused	entertained	irritated

Activity 3

Developing your ideas

1 Look carefully at the poem's rhymes and stanza structure. What do you notice about them? Why do you think the poet has crafted his poem in this way?

2 The poem contrasts images of youthfulness with thoughts of time passing, and death. (This is similar to techniques used by Andrew Marvell in 'To His Coy Mistress', see page 78).

Look at the following table, and match the writer's technique to an example, and the intended effect on the reader.

Writer's technique	Example	Effect on the reader
Descriptions of warmth associated with youth	'The sooner will his race be run, / And nearer he's to setting.'	Appears to be helpful advice, pointing out that while we have time we should make the most of it.
Instructions to the reader	'Gather ye'	Uses words associated with passion, so this links youth with enjoyment and love.
Images of the day ending to suggest the ending of life	'When youth and blood are warmer'	An effective image to show that youth and beauty are fleeting.
Clear recommendations about how to behave	'And this same flower that smiles today, / Tomorrow will be dying.'	Makes the poem seem more forceful and suggests urgency.
Personification of youth through associating it with the natural world	'Then be not coy, but use your time'	Reminds the reader that the sun has a cycle much like human life. It also links with the idea of warmth and strength being associated with youth.

Activity 4

Developing a personal response

1 How do you respond to the poem? Do you think it makes a good point, or that this carpe diem (seize the day) attitude towards male/female relationships could cause difficulties? (You might like to look at the situation in 'The Beggar Woman' by William King, see page 82.) Give reasons and support your ideas with evidence from the text.

2 The closing lines seem to offer a thought about old age. Discuss what you think they mean.

Peer/Self-assessment

1 Answer true or false to the following statements.
I can find evidence for and comment on:
- a the way youth is shown as beautiful in the poem
- b the way life is seen as being very short
- c the way the poet uses images from the natural world to make his point
- d how the poet seems to encourage the reader to 'seize the day'
- e how the poem suggests that old age is not so enjoyable as youth
- f my response to the poem.

2 If you answered 'false' to any statements, compare your ideas with a partner's. Look again at the poem and your answers to the questions on these pages to help you.

3 a Write two paragraphs responding to the task:
How does Herrick present male/female relationships in 'To the Virgins, To Make Much of Time'?

b Look at the grade descriptors on pages 148–155. What grade would you award your response?

To His Coy Mistress

by Andrew Marvell

My learning objectives

- to explore the themes of the poem, including male/female relationships
- to develop my response to Marvell's poem
- to assess my work on Marvell's poem against the criteria in Assessment Objective 2 (page 134).

GradeStudio

Examiner tips

You can achieve a high grade if you:

- make detailed reference to the language and structure Marvell uses to convey the narrator's thoughts
- use well-chosen quotations from the poem to support your points on theme, content, language and structure
- explore comparisons and links you can make between this poem about men and women and other texts with similar themes.

First thoughts

Activity 1

This poem is persuading someone to do something. What different strategies do you notice the narrator using? Do these change in its three sections?

Looking more closely

Activity 2

1 Look at the descriptions and images. Why do you think the poet selects the following? Copy and complete the table.

Image	What it means	Why it is used
'Indian Ganges' side'		
'rubies'		
'An hundred years should go to praise / Thine eyes'		

2 Look at the following lines:

'But at my back I always hear
Time's wingèd chariot hurrying near;
And yonder all before us lie
Deserts of vast eternity.'

a How does this part of the poem show a change of attitude in the narrator? What is he saying here?

b Why do you think he uses the images of a 'wingèd chariot' and endless desert?

3 The narrator then tries even stronger tactics to persuade his mistress that time is running out. In the table below, match the description of his tactics with the appropriate quotation and its effect.

Narrator's tactics	Quotation	Effect
Flatters her	'Two hundred to adore each breast'	Accepts that privacy is desirable, but emphasises the loneliness of death
Reminds her that time is running out	'Nor, in thy marble vault, shall sound / My echoing song'	A sense of loneliness and bleakness, underlined by the use of different senses
Tries to frighten her about the coldness and loneliness of death	'The grave's a fine and private place / But none, I think, do there embrace.'	Suggests speed, and that time is literally flying away
Tries to disgust her with the idea of wasting her virginity	'Time's wingèd chariot hurrying near'	A grotesque image designed to shock, and make her think of the waste of her beauty
Half-pretends to agree with her feelings of reserve	'then worms shall try / That long-preserved virginity'	Deliberate exaggeration. Has moved on from admiring her eyes to her breasts (a more private part)

Developing your ideas

Activity 3

1 In the last part, the narrator describes his ideas about a solution. The images are very striking. They could be divided into 'passionate', 'short-lived', and 'violent' images. Look through the final 14 lines (33–46) and decide whether each image fits any of these categories, giving reasons why.

2 How seriously are we intended to take the narrator's ideas in this poem? Comment on some examples of his teasing wit.

Developing a personal response

Activity 4

Students have given the following responses to the poem. Select two you agree with and two you disagree with. For each, find evidence from the poem to support your view.

Student A

'This poem is all about desire and passion rather than real love.'

Student B

'The poem is a romantic portrayal of love between the sexes.'

Student C

'The narrator is unlikely to persuade any woman with such arguments; she will see through his posturing.'

Student D

'The narrator doesn't really seem to desire the woman; instead, he is enjoying being clever.'

Student E

'The most impressive thing about the poem is the use of fanciful imagery.'

Poem Glossary

Coyness: pretending to be shy
Indian Ganges: sacred river in India
Complain: express pain or resentment
Conversion of the Jews: event that will not happen until the end of time
Eternity: the state or time after death
Marble: stone
Vault: a burial chamber
Quaint: over-fastidious
Hue: colour
Transpires: breathes
Amorous: loving
Slow-chapt: slowly chewing
Strife: struggle or violent effort

Peer/Self-assessment

MAKE THE GRADE

1 Read this paragraph, written in response to the task:
How does Marvell present male/female relationships in 'To His Coy Mistress'?

2 Write a paragraph giving your own response to the task. Use the same structure as the paragraph on the right.

3 Annotate your paragraph using the same notes as the paragraph on the right. If you have forgotten to include anything in your paragraph, add it in.

4 Which criteria in Assessment Objective 2 on page 134 have you demonstrated in your paragraph?

A clear point

Evidence to support the point

The poem starts in a highly romantic and extravagant manner:
'Thou by the Indian Ganges' side
Shouldst rubies find'.
Here he uses the exotic nature of India to suggest the precious nature of his love. The image of the rubies suggests richness and pleasant surprises. However, the narrator is already saying that this is not possible. He starts off saying 'Had we' and 'We would' – in reality he is offering something much less romantic.

An explanation of the effect of the quotation

How language reflects the poet's point of view

Close focus on the writer's choice of language

Song: The Willing Mistriss

by Aphra Behn

My learning objectives

- to explore the themes of the poem, including male/female relationships
- to develop my response to Behn's poem
- to assess my work on Behn's poem against the criteria in Assessment Objective 2 (page 134).

GradeStudio

MAKE THE GRADE MAKE THE GRADE

Examiner tips

You can achieve a high grade if you:

- make detailed reference to the language and structure Behn uses to convey the narrator's thoughts
- use well-chosen quotations from the poem to support your points on theme, content, language and structure
- explore comparisons and links you can make between this poem about men and women and other texts with similar themes.

Poem Glossary

Grove: group of trees
Though: even if
Strove: tried
Betrayed: given away
Secur'd: safe
Yielding: giving way
Boughs: branches
Amorous: romantic and loving
Tricks: games
Aid: help
Prevaile: succeed in persuading
Clasp: hold, embrace
Express: told

First thoughts

Activity 1

1 Look at the poem's title.
   a What sort of poem does the title indicate it will be?
   b What does it suggest will happen?

2 Summarise what happens in the poem in two short sentences. Thinking about the themes of this poem and the language used, consider which other poems you have read with a similar theme.

Looking more closely

Activity 2

1 There are many **pastoral** (nature) descriptions. Choose at least four. For each, explain the techniques used and explain why you think the poet uses them. For example:

   The wind is personified – it kisses 'the yielding Boughs'. The fact that nature is acting in a romantic and passionate way increases the anticipation in the poem. It also indicates what the young couple will do next.

2 What tone do you think this poem has? In pairs, discuss which of the following words best describe the overall attitude of the narrator. Find evidence from the text to support your ideas.

serious	cheerful	bitter	light-hearted
solemn	ironic	joyful	happy
thoughtful	depressed	romantic	boastful
carefree	optimistic	remorseful	distressed

Developing your ideas

Activity 3

1 The poem ends with a question addressed to the reader. Why does the poet decide to do this?

2 Look at how the relationship is described. Which of the following statements are true and which are false? Find evidence to support your ideas.
   - Amyntas is a romantic lover.
   - The relationship is more focused on lust than love.
   - The woman in the poem needs a lot of persuasion by the man.
   - The relationship is described as a very physical and passionate one.
   - It seems like an equal relationship between the partners.

Activity 4

Developing a personal response

1 The writer has used various poetic techniques. Copy the following table, matching the writer's technique with the example. Then explain what effect each has on you as a reader.

Technique	Example	Effect created
Personification of the natural world	'On her that was already fir'd'	
Hyperbole (extravagant and obvious exaggeration)	'The Sun it self, though it had Strove, / It could not have betray'd us'	
Euphemism (hinting at something embarrassing or shocking)	'A Thousand Amorous Tricks'	
Images associated with heat and fire	'That which I dare not name.'	

2 How do you respond to the situation in the poem? Do you think it portrays a serious relationship? Why do you think Aphra Behn (a female poet) decided to write the poem as a dramatic monologue from the woman's viewpoint?

3 a Aphra Behn was writing poetry in the 1600s. At that time, women were not expected to have the same attitudes as men towards passionate relationships. In pairs, explain how this poem challenges traditional views of women.

b Write a paragraph explaining how the woman in this poem is presented. You might compare the way women are portrayed in other poems, such as 'To His Coy Mistress' (see page 74) and 'The Beggar Woman' (see page 82).

Peer/Self-assessment

MAKE THE GRADE

1 Read this paragraph written in response to the task:

How does Behn present male/female relationships in 'The Willing Mistriss'?

2 Write a paragraph giving your own response to the task. Use the same structure as the paragraph on the right.

3 Annotate your paragraph using the same notes as the paragraph on the right. If you have forgotten to include anything in your paragraph, add it in.

4 Which criteria in Assessment Objective 2 on page 134 have you demonstrated in your paragraph?

Evidence used to support the point

A clear point

Behn presents an incident where both the man and the woman act in a passionate way:
'A many Kisses he did give:
And I return'd the same'.
The poem is unusual because the woman seems to act as readily as the man; she relishes his attentions. This is shown by the words 'I return'd', suggesting she is as lustful as the man. The poet writes in the first person, which makes us feel close to the woman's thoughts and feelings.

An explanation of the effect of the quotation

How language reflects the poet's point of view

Close focus on the writer's choice of language

A Woman to Her Lover

by Christina Walsh

My learning objectives

- to explore the themes of the poem, including male/female relationships
- to develop my response to Walsh's poem
- to assess my work on Walsh's poem against the criteria in Assessment Objective 2 (page 134).

GradeStudio

MAKE THE GRADE MAKE THE GRADE

Examiner tips

You can achieve a high grade if you:

- make detailed reference to the language and structure Walsh uses to convey the narrator's thoughts
- use well-chosen quotations from the poem to support your points on theme, content, language and structure
- explore comparisons and links you can make between this poem about men and women and other texts with similar themes.

Poem Glossary

Vanquished: defeated
Bondslave: slave or servant
Drudgery: dull, harsh or boring work
Feeble: weak or pathetic
Gratify: please or satisfy
Clamorous: demanding
Caresses: loving touches
Abasement: degradation or humiliation
Wakened: enlightened, liberated
Spheres: heavens
Fugue: musical form with interweaving parts

First thoughts

Activity 1

1. In this poem a woman explains what she wants (and does not want) from marriage. Write down five characteristics you think an ideal marriage should have. For example:

   Equality – both should help with household chores.

2. Think about any marriages you have seen on television or in fiction that you would not like to be part of. What makes them fall short of the ideal marriage?

Looking more closely

Activity 2

1. The woman is the only speaker, which makes this poem a dramatic monologue. In pairs, practise reading the poem aloud with an appropriate tone for each section.
   What do you notice about how this changes?
2. What impression do you get of the woman's personality from the way she speaks?
3. Look at the descriptions of different types of relationships. Which of the following statements can you find evidence for in the poem?
   - She does not want to be told what to do.
   - She does not want to be responsible for all domestic chores.
   - She wants equality more than anything else.
   - She thinks she is as good as her partner.
   - She is a strong and independent woman.
   - She sees marriage as an adventure.

4 The narrator reveals her attitude towards marriage in her imagery. In the table below, match the image with the appropriate quotation and meaning.

Image of a wife	Quotation	Meaning
A slave or servant to the man	'your comrade, friend, and mate, / To live and work, to love and die with you'	The word 'creature' suggests a loss of intellect and emotion; existing only to please him physically
A glorified but shallow object for the man to admire	'A creature who will have no greater joy / Than gratify your clamorous desire'	The perfect blend of passion and friendship; a balanced and fulfilling relationship
A pet or belonging of the man	'A wingless angel who can do no wrong / Go! – I am no doll to dress and sit for feeble worship'	A relationship that involves being defeated by a man and placed in slavery
A partner and soulmate	'As conqueror to the vanquished / To make of me a bondslave'	Pampered and pretty girls are like beautiful angels but are 'wingless', which suggests they have no independence

Developing your ideas

Activity 3

1 The poem builds up pictures of different male/female relationships. How convincing do you find these pictures of different types of marriages?

2 The poet uses striking vocabulary to express her views about relationships. Choose four individual words that interest you, and explain why.

Developing a personal response

Activity 4

In pairs, discuss your response to the poem and the effectiveness of the:

- layout and structure
- use of imagery
- narrative viewpoint (is it effective to hear only the woman's?)
- use of the senses.

Peer/Self-assessment

1 Read this paragraph, written in response to the task:

How does Walsh present male/female relationships in 'A Woman to Her Lover'?

2 Write a paragraph giving your own response to the task. Use the same structure as the paragraph on the right.

3 Annotate your paragraph using the same notes as the paragraph on the right. If you have forgotten to include anything in your paragraph, add it in.

4 Which criteria in Assessment Objective 2 on page 134 have you demonstrated in your paragraph?

A clear point

Evidence to support the point

The narrator shows that many relationships are full of inequality:
'My skin soft only for your fond caresses
My body supple only for your sense delight'.
The repeated word 'only' indicates that he regards her beauty as being just for his benefit. The description of touch in 'caresses' and 'sense delight' suggests a marriage based on shallow physical enjoyment for the man. A wife is seen here as a mere object, and the narrator goes on to reject this.

Close focus on the writer's choice of language

How language reflects the poet's point of view

An explanation of the effect of the quotation

My learning objectives

- to explore the themes of the poem, including male/female relationships
- to develop my response to Heaney's poem
- to assess my work on Heaney's poem against the criteria in Assessment Objective 2 (page 134).

GradeStudio

Examiner tips

You can achieve a high grade if you:

- make detailed reference to the language and structure Heaney uses to convey the narrator's thoughts
- use well-chosen quotations from the poem to support your points on theme, content, language and structure
- explore comparisons and links you can make between this poem about men and women and other texts with similar themes.

Poem Glossary

À la Bardot: in the style of Brigitte Bardot, a glamorous film star in the 1950s and 1960s
Diaphragm: muscular structure separating the chest from the abdomen
Backcloth: painted curtain at the back of a stage
Tremulous: trembling or quivering
Vacuum: completely empty space
Decorum: proper behaviour, following society's rules
Deployed: unfolded strategically
Juvenilia: works produced at a young age; youthful experiences
Chary: cautious, wary

Twice Shy

by Seamus Heaney

Activity 1

First thoughts

1 Imagine a time ten years in the future. You are in your mid twenties, and you are going on a date. Think about how you might feel about it. What might your hopes be? What might be your concerns and worries? Spend two minutes noting down all your ideas.

2 Why might it be more nerve-racking or difficult going on a date when you are older, compared to your teenage years? What clues about this do you notice in 'Twice Shy'?

Activity 2

Looking more closely

1 Re-read stanzas 1 and 2. It describes the couple going on a walk by the river.
   a How does the poet describe the woman?
   b How does the poet try to make the surroundings seem full of tension and awkwardness?

2 Look again at the beginning of stanza 3:
   'A vacuum of need
   Collapsed each hunting heart
   But tremulously we held
   As hawk and prey apart'
   Discuss with your partner what you think these lines mean. Write down three things you would like to ask about these lines. Then discuss your questions with another pair.

3 The couple both appear to have had other, failed relationships. Look carefully at the following image:
   'Mushroom loves already
   Had puffed and burst in hate.'
   a Why do you think the writer chooses the image of overripe mushrooms to describe past unsuccessful relationships?
   b Choose one word in the quotation above and explain why you think it has been used.

4 There are many bird images in the poem. Look at each of them and think about why they have been used. Is it clear which of the couple is the hawk (the hunter) and which the thrush (the hunted)? Give reasons for your answer.

Developing your ideas

Activity 3

1 Look carefully at the end of the poem. Do you think the couple's date has been a success? Give reasons for your answer.

2 Think about the title of the poem. There is a common saying, 'Once bitten, twice shy.' Does this help explain any aspect of the poem?

3 If you were asked to give the poem an alternative title, what would you choose? Explain your choice.

Developing a personal response

Activity 4

1 Students have made the following comments about the poem. Decide whether you agree or disagree with each point, finding evidence from the poem to support your ideas.

Student A

'The most interesting thing about this poem is the way Heaney uses the surroundings to show the mixture of excitement and awkwardness the couple feel.'

Student B

'The river is the most important image in the poem – it suggests the hidden depths and emotions that are going on under the surface in each person.'

Student C

'I find the bird images disturbing. The image of hunting seems strange in a poem about a new relationship.'

Student D

'The bird images are the cleverest thing about the poem. They show that it is unclear which of the couple has dominance. Also, although they act and speak politely, there are undercurrents of passion and power.'

2 How successful do you think Heaney is in capturing interactions between men and women at the start of a relationship? Give reasons for your answers.

Peer/Self-assessment

1 Write two paragraphs responding to the task:
How are male/female relationships presented in 'Twice Shy'?

2 Look at the grade descriptors on pages 148–155. What grade would you award your response?

3 What could you change or add to improve your grade? Use the grade descriptors to identify the two things most likely to improve your grade.

4 Redraft your answer, trying to make those changes.

5 Look again at the grade descriptors. Have you improved your grade?

My learning objectives

- to explore the themes of the poem, including male/female relationships
- to develop my response to King's poem
- to assess my work on King's poem against the criteria in Assessment Objective 2 (page 134).

GradeStudio

Examiner tips

You can achieve a high grade if you:

- make detailed reference to the language and structure King uses to convey the poem's message
- use well-chosen quotations from the poem to support your points on theme, content, language and structure
- explore comparisons and links that you can make between this poem about men and women and other texts with similar themes.

Poem Glossary

Astray: away from the correct path
Retire: retreat
Courtship: persuading a woman to accept romantic interest
Hinders: holds back
Thither: here
Squire: wealthy man
Use: habit
Disoblige: inconvenience
Burthen: burden or weight
Dextrous: skilful
Ere you get another: before you father another

The Beggar Woman

by William King

Activity 1

First thoughts

1. This poem is about the difficulties of being an unemployed woman with a baby and no partner. It is set over 300 years ago. In pairs, jot down the difficulties that such a woman might face. How might the situation be different for the man who made her pregnant?
2. Look at what this man says to the beggar woman. What does he appear to be suggesting? Why might the woman be less keen on this?

Activity 2

Looking more closely

1. Look carefully at the description of the beggar woman. How does the poet make her sound attractive?
2. How does the woman react when the man first makes his offer?
3. She gives a reason why she can't leave the baby on the ground. What is this?
4. Discuss the following line with a partner:
   'Mighty well, sir! Oh, Lord! if tied to you!'
5. The woman acts in an unusual way as she ties her baby onto the man's back. Look carefully at the words that describe this action:
   'With speed incredible to work she goes,
   And from her shoulders soon the burthen throws;
   Then mounts the infant with a gentle toss
   Upon her generous friend, and, like a cross,
   The sheet she with a dextrous motion winds'
   a. How do you think the woman feels about her baby?
   b. Why do you think she ties the sheet 'like a cross'? What might this suggest?

Activity 3

Developing your ideas

1. Think about the poem as a whole. Students have made the following comments. Decide whether you agree or disagree with each, and find evidence to support your opinion.

Student A

'This poem shows that men often have the power in a relationship. The man is only concerned with his own desires.'

Student B

'The woman gets the upper hand in this situation. She shows the man what a terrible burden can result from a "bit of fun".'

Student C

'King shows the power struggle in relationships. He shows that men are only interested in sex and do anything to get their own way.'

Student D

'This poem shows that although women have less physical strength than men, they can often get their own way through cunning and manipulation.'

Student E

'This poem is still relevant today. It shows the dangers of casual and unprotected sex.'

2 The poem is set out like a story; it is a narrative poem. Various devices and descriptions add to its interest. In pairs, discuss the choices King has made then copy and complete the table below – the first entry has been done for you.

Poet's device	Effect	Why it has been chosen
Tells a complete story	Creates interest for the reader, as it shows the two characters meeting and hints at what the man hopes for. Ends dramatically with the woman outsmarting the man	To hold the reader's interest by telling an entertaining story with a beginning, middle and end
Includes plenty of physical description, of both the setting and the characters		
Quotes the speech of the characters		
The last two lines rhyme and sound like a moral		

Developing a personal response

1 How successful do you think King is in presenting an interesting incident between a man and woman?

2 If the squire met the woman again a year later, what do you think he would say about his experience? Would his attitudes towards lower-class women and casual sex have changed as a result of this encounter? Find evidence from the poem for his current attitude. Write a few lines describing his feelings a year later.

Peer/Self-assessment

1 Write two paragraphs responding to the task:
How are male/female relationships presented in 'The Beggar Woman'?

2 Look at the grade descriptors on pages 148–155. What grade would you award your response?

3 What could you change or add to improve your grade? Use the grade descriptors to identify the two things most likely to improve your grade.

4 Redraft your answer, trying to make those changes.

5 Look again at the grade descriptors. Have you improved your grade?

Whoso List to Hunt

by Sir Thomas Wyatt

My learning objectives

- to explore the themes of the poem, including male/female relationships
- to develop my response to Wyatt's poem
- to assess my work on Wyatt's poem against the criteria in Assessment Objective 2 (page 134).

GradeStudio

Examiner tips

You can achieve a high grade if you:

- make detailed reference to the language and structure Wyatt uses to convey the narrator's thoughts
- use well-chosen quotations from the poem to support your points on theme, content, language and structure
- explore comparisons and links you can make between this poem about men and women and other texts with similar themes.

Poem Glossary

Whoso list: whoever wishes
Hind: female deer
Alas: exclamation of pain or despair
Vain travail: hopeless effort
Hath wearied: has exhausted
Sore: painfully
Fleeth afore: runs ahead
Graven: engraved
Noli me tangere: Latin motto meaning 'do not touch me'

First thoughts

Activity 1

1 This poem compares a man's efforts to win the love of a woman to a hunt for a beautiful deer. Describing the pursuit of love as being like a hunt is a common image in poetry and life. Explain in two sentences the links you can find between hunting and male/female relationships.

2 a Other poems in this collection refer to hunting and catching 'prey'. Can you name any?
  b In this poem, who is the hunter and who is hunted? Find evidence from the poem to support your ideas.

Looking more closely

Activity 2

1 This poem is spoken by a narrator. Who do you think is the 'voice' of the poem? What clues can you find out about his relationship with the woman?

2 What impression do you gain of the woman who is depicted as the 'hind'? Add to the following mind map:

'she fleeth afore'
Perhaps she does not want to be caught and is just teasing him?

'fair neck'
Suggests that she is beautiful and feminine.

Beautiful deer = Woman

'for Caesar's I am'
Suggests that she belongs to another. Caesar suggests a wealthy, rich man. Perhaps even royalty?

3 Look carefully at the poem and decide what you think its mood is. For example, do you think it has a hopeful mood because the narrator is enjoying the hunt? Or do you see the mood as depressed and deflated? Choose two adjectives from the list below and use evidence from the poem to support your ideas.

hopeful	joyful	proud	disappointed
distressed	fearful	doubtful	cold-hearted
exhausted	worried	jealous	exhilarated
excited	expectant	secretive	spiteful
resigned	lonely	thoughtful	guilty
remorseful			

Developing your ideas

Activity 3

1 The poet uses a number of images and poetic devices to put his ideas across. In the table below, match the poet's technique, the example and its intended effect.

Technique	Example	Effect
Direct address to the reader	'deer'	An impossible task, to highlight how he feels about hunting the beautiful deer
Repetition of key words	'Whoso list to hunt, I know where is an hind'	Means 'hopeless' or 'futile'; its repetition emphasises how dejected he feels
Image of a difficult capture	'Wearied me so sore' 'Fainting I follow'	'deer' sounds like 'dear', a beloved or special person; shows his feelings for the woman
Pun (play on words)	'Since in a net I seek to hold the wind'	Highlights his desperation; he is ready to give up the chase as he is mentally and physically exhausted
Words associated with exhaustion	'vain'	Gains the reader's attention immediately; he is talking to us and sharing a secret

2 Wyatt was a member of the group of rich young people at the court of Henry VIII in the 1530s. Henry VIII had recently decided to divorce Catherine of Aragon in order to marry the young, beautiful and popular Anne Boleyn. Hunting deer in the royal forest was a popular pastime.

Does any of this background information help your understanding of the poem? Write two sentences explaining your thoughts.

3 Can you find any references to royalty, power, or court life in the poem?

Developing a personal response

Activity 4

1 Is 'Whoso List to Hunt' a poem about a) true love, b) unrequited love, c) equal relationships, or d) obsessive love? In pairs, decide which category it fits best. Explain your reasons in three sentences.

2 Imagine the woman is writing a reply to the poet. How does she feel about the situation? Find clues in the poem about the type of life she leads. Write a few lines showing how the woman might present her views on male/female relationships.

Peer/Self-assessment

1 Write two paragraphs responding to the task:
How are male/female relationships presented in 'Whoso List to Hunt'?

2 Look at the grade descriptors on pages 148–155. What grade would you award your response?

3 What could you change or add to improve your grade? Use the grade descriptors to identify the two things most likely to improve your grade.

4 Redraft your answer, trying to make those changes.

5 Look again at the grade descriptors. Have you improved your grade?

My learning objectives

- to explore the themes of the poem, including male/female relationships
- to develop my response to Shakespeare's sonnet
- to assess my work on Shakespeare's sonnet against the criteria in Assessment Objective 2 (page 134).

GradeStudio

MAKE THE GRADE

Examiner tips

You can achieve a high grade if you:

- make detailed reference to the language and structure Shakespeare uses to convey the narrator's thoughts
- use well-chosen quotations from the poem to support your points on theme, content, language and structure
- explore comparisons and links that you can make between this poem about men and women and other texts with similar themes.

Sonnet 116

by William Shakespeare

Activity 1

First thoughts

1 Discuss with your partner the five qualities you think are required in a perfect love relationship. Write a couple of lines of poetry that express these.

2 Look at these two lines of the sonnet:

'Love is not love
Which alters when it alteration finds'

Discuss with your partner what you think the poet means here.

Activity 2

Looking more closely

1 This sonnet describes a perfect and long-lasting love. Shakespeare uses a range of images and ideas to describe how true love lasts, and not just in the good times; lovers can face together the difficulties of life.

Copy and complete the following table, making notes on what is interesting about each image, and what the words suggest to you.

Image	What is interesting about it	What it suggests
'it is an ever-fixed mark, / That looks on tempests and is never shaken'	Image of a permanent beacon or signal like a lighthouse that keeps ships safe in the stormy seas	'Ever-fixed' suggests it is everlasting; a romantic image, as true love is thought to be endless. The stormy seas suggest life's difficulties
'though rosy lips and cheeks / Within his bending sickle's compass come'		
'Love alters not with his brief hours and weeks'		
'But bears it out even to the edge of doom.'		

Developing your ideas

Activity 3

1 a This sonnet focuses on love's steadiness in the face of change and the passing of time. Pick out the references to time that are related to:
- ageing
- the end of time itself
- movement or travel.

b Why has Shakespeare chosen these images when he is trying to show that true love is unchanging?

2 Look carefully at the final couplet:
'If this be error and upon me proved,
I never writ, nor no man ever loved.'
What do you think these lines mean? Is the poet completely convinced by this view of true love, or could it be that he thinks his comments in the rest of the poem are extravagant, and he is making a less optimistic assessment here?

Poem Glossary

Impediments: objections
Alteration: change
Ever-fixed mark: permanent beacon or signal for shipping
Tempests: storms (especially at sea)
Wandering bark: lost ship
Sickle: tool with a sharp blade for cutting crops
Compass: reach
Doom: Doomsday, the end of time

Developing a personal response

Activity 4

Students have written the following notes on their responses to the poem. Which do you agree with, and which do you disagree with? For each, find evidence from the poem to support your view.

Student A
'This poem is suitable to be read at a wedding, celebrating love and lasting relationships.'

Student B
'It is about the resilience and strength of true love.'

Student C
'It is romantic, but realistic. It shows that love and life do not always run smoothly.'

Student D
'It is about both young and mature love.'

Student E
'It is unrealistic. Love is bound to change with time and the stresses of life.'

Student F
'It emphasises the effects of time because it is showing that love can survive all changes and challenges.'

Student G
'The ending shows Shakespeare's belief in what he has written.'

Peer/Self-assessment

1 Read this paragraph, written in response to the task:
How does Shakespeare present male/female relationships in 'Sonnet 116'?

2 Write a paragraph giving your own response to the task. Use the same structure as the paragraph on the right.

3 Annotate your paragraph using the same notes as the paragraph above. If you have forgotten to include anything in your paragraph, add it in.

4 Which criteria in Assessment Objective 2 on page 134 have you demonstrated in your paragraph?

Evidence to support the point | A clear point

The sonnet suggests that true love is constant and unchanging:
'Love's not Time's fool, though rosy lips and cheeks
Within his bending sickle's compass come'.
These lines show that time does have an effect – it can destroy the freshness of beauty. This is shown by the image of 'rosy cheeks' being harvested by the 'sickle', an image of time passing and youth ending. But the point is that even though lovers will age, their love can remain true.

An explanation of the effect of the quotation | How the language reflects the poet's point of view | Close focus on the writer's choice of language

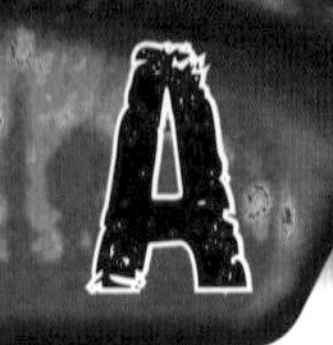

Sonnet 130

by William Shakespeare

My learning objectives

- to explore the themes of the poem, including male/female relationships
- to develop my response to Shakespeare's sonnet
- to assess my work on Shakespeare's sonnet against the criteria in Assessment Objective 2 (page 134).

GradeStudio

Examiner tips

You can achieve a high grade if you:

- make detailed reference to the language and structure Shakespeare uses to convey the narrator's thoughts
- use well-chosen quotations from the poem to support your points on theme, content, language and structure
- explore comparisons and links you can make between this poem about men and women and other texts with similar themes.

Poem Glossary

Coral: semi-precious pink or red substance from the sea, used in jewellery
Wires: finely spun thread
Dun: greyish brown
Damask'd: patterned; also, a Damask rose is pink or red
Reeks: breathes
Any she: any woman
Belied: lied about, falsified
Compare: comparison

Activity 1

First thoughts

In typical love poems, greetings cards and romantic films, what sort of comments and descriptions are usually made about a woman who is loved? How is this poem different?

Activity 2

Looking more closely

1 This sonnet, like many of Shakespeare's, is addressed to the mysterious Dark Lady. It describes his mistress without flattery. Read through the poem and find examples of where he describes her in a less than romantic light. Discuss why you think the poet might describe her in such a way.

2 Copy and complete the following table about the language of the sonnet.

Comment on his mistress	What this means	Its effect
'eyes are nothing like the sun'	Her eyes don't in any way resemble the sun. They are not shiny and dazzling. Eyes are often praised in love poetry, and compared to the sun or stars	Very direct. It is shocking to see such a negative comparison
'her breasts are dun'		
'black wires grow on her head'		
'music hath a far more pleasing sound'		
'when she walks, treads on the ground'		

3 a The last couplet in the sonnet seems to explain everything. With a partner, and using the Glossary, discuss what you think they mean:
'And yet, by heaven, I think my love as rare
As any she belied with false compare.'

b Why do you think that Shakespeare chooses to end the sonnet in this way?

Activity 3

Developing your ideas

1 Readers have different views of the narrator's response to his mistress. Look at the following words used to describe his attitude, and choose three that you most agree with and two you totally disagree with. Find examples from the sonnet to support your ideas.

jealous	hurtful	realistic	honest	optimistic	loving
unkind	spiteful	truthful	hateful	humorous	realistic
romantic	passionate	boastful	serious	light-hearted	dishonest

2 The sonnet makes use of the five senses. Choose three images that involve different senses, and describe them as in the following example. Comment on the language used.

The sense of touch. The mistress is described as walking: 'I never saw a goddess go, / My mistress, when she walks, treads on the ground'.

The narrator does not claim she moves like a 'goddess', supposedly with a smooth, gliding motion. Instead she is described as being literally down to earth – she simply walks on the normal 'ground'.

Activity 4

Developing a personal response

Look at the two statements below. With a partner, take turns in finding as much supporting evidence as you can for each view.

Student A:

This is a very truthful poem about relationships and love. It is actually more romantic than many traditional love poems, as the poet is open and honest about his mistress. He knows that she isn't perfect, but he loves her anyway. Surely this is the most romantic thing of all?

Student B:

This poem misses the point about male/female relationships. When you are in love your lover should be seen as perfect and amazing. Looking at love too realistically ruins this. This poem doesn't work because it destroys the romance and magic of love. Relationships don't develop if we see our partner's flaws too clearly.

Peer/Self-assessment

1 Read this paragraph, written in response to the task:

How does Shakespeare present male/female relationships in 'Sonnet 130'?

2 Write a paragraph giving your own response to the task. Use the same structure as the paragraph on the right.

3 Annotate your paragraph using the same notes as the paragraph on the right. If you have forgotten to include anything in your paragraph, add it in.

4 Which of the criteria in Assessment Objective 2 on page 134 have you demonstrated in your paragraph?

A clear point

Evidence to support the point

The poet presents relationships in a very truthful, even blunt fashion:
'If hairs be wires, black wires grow on her head.'
Here he emphasises the dark colour of his mistress's hair. Blonde hair was prized in those days and highlighting her darkness with the word 'black' is unflattering. This shows the poet's honesty and vivid visual description.

An explanation of the effect of the quotation

How the language reflects the poet's point of view

Close focus on the writer's choice of language

Song of the Worker's Wife

by Alice Gray Jones

My learning objectives

- to explore the themes of the poem, including male/female relationships
- to develop my response to Jones's poem
- to assess my work on Jones's poem against the criteria in Assessment Objective 2 (page 134).

GradeStudio

Examiner tips

You can achieve a high grade if you:

- make detailed reference to the language and structure Jones uses to convey the narrator's thoughts
- use well-chosen quotations from the poem to support your points on theme, content, language and structure
- explore comparisons and links you can make between this poem about men and women and other texts with similar themes.

Poem Glossary

Labour: hard, manual work
Chores: everyday household jobs
Workbox: container for sewing materials
Initiative: ability to take responsibility

Activity 1

First thoughts

1 This poem is about the care and work a mother gives to her family.
  a Look at the following periods in a child's life. For each, spend one minute listing all the things a mother might do to care for a child. For example, babies need feeding, bathing, dressing, etc.
  • Newborn baby • Child under five • School child • Teenager
  What do you notice about each list?
  b If you completed the same activity for fathers' tasks, would it be similar or different?
2 The poem was written some time ago. Find at least three pieces of evidence from the text to show it is not a contemporary poem.

Activity 2

Looking more closely

1 The mother is speaking in the poem, and she appears to take a great deal of pride in the housework she completes. Find at least three pieces of evidence for this and explain each one. For example:
  She describes the newly washed clothes as 'snow white clothes all aired'. Describing them as being like snow makes them sound really white and pure.
2 The children are mentioned throughout the poem. What do you find out about them?
3 Is there much description of the father in the poem? Why do you think this is? What evidence can you find about him and his relationship with his wife and family?

Developing your ideas

Activity 3

1 Think about the poem as a whole. Students have made the following comments. Decide whether you agree or disagree with each comment, and find evidence to support your ideas.

Student A

'This poem celebrates family life and shows the joy women can experience in caring for others.'

Student B

'Although the woman in the poem says she enjoys her life, the ending is troubling. She has invested all her energy and time in her children and once they are grown, she is old and redundant.'

Student C

'This poem is a truthful representation of the drudgery of many women's lives. I don't think the poet is suggesting that we should want to live like this. The last stanza offers a warning about the future for women who live purely for others.'

Student D

'The most interesting thing about this poem is the lack of description of the husband and his role in the house. It seems that the only love in the poem is that of the mother for her children.'

2 How do you respond to this poem? Write your opinion in a paragraph and include at least one quotation to support your points.

3 The poet has chosen to use particular features. Read the poem aloud and discuss the following:

- the rhythm, and what this adds to its meaning
- the fact that much of the poem is written in the past tense, and the effect of this
- the imagery of birds and nesting throughout the poem
- the fact that most of the poem is written in simple, everyday language.

Developing a personal response

Activity 4

1 The wife doesn't complain about the endless chores she completes. Do you think this is realistic? Find two parts of the poem that you find particularly convincing or unconvincing, and give your reasons for choosing them.

2 a Imagine that you could ask the wife in the poem two questions about her life. What would you ask? What questions do you have about her relationship with her husband?

b Now think of two questions you might ask the poet. For example, you might ask whether Jones intended to present the woman as being happy with her life, even though it involves such hard work without reward.

Peer/Self-assessment

1 Write two paragraphs responding to the task:
How are male/female relationships presented in 'Song of the Worker's Wife'?

2 Look at the grade descriptors on pages 148–155. What grade would you award your response?

3 What could you change or add to improve your grade? Use the grade descriptors to identify the two things most likely to improve your grade.

4 Redraft your answer, trying to make those changes.

5 Look again at the grade descriptors. Have you improved your grade?

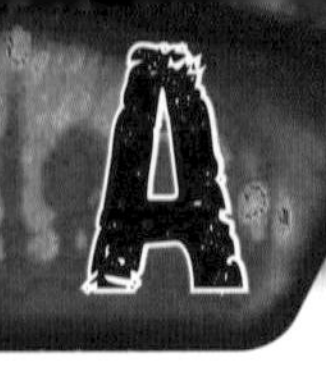

A Married State

by Katherine Philips

My learning objectives

- to explore the themes of the poem, including male/female relationships
- to develop my response to Philips's poem
- to assess my work on Philips's poem against the criteria in Assessment Objective 2 (page 134).

GradeStudio

MAKE THE GRADE

Examiner tips

You can achieve a high grade if you:

- make detailed reference to the language and structure Philips uses to convey the narrator's thoughts
- use well-chosen quotations from the poem to support your points on theme, content, language and structure
- explore comparisons and links you can make between this poem about men and women and other texts with similar themes.

Poem Glossary

Desemble: conceal
Blustering: raging or bullying
Extort: wring out
Matrimony: marriage
Apostate: person who abandons a religion or principle
Levity: frivolousness or temptation
Supress: crush or hold down
Leading apes in hell: traditionally said to be the punishment after death for women who remain unmarried

First thoughts

Activity 1

Practise reading 'A Married State' in different ways. What sort of tone and attitude do you think the speaker has? Experiment with making the narrator sound very serious, humorous, angry, or concerned. Which approach do you think is best suited to this poem? Give reasons why.

Looking more closely

Activity 2

1 This poem details some of the disadvantages of being married. For each example below, explain what it means, then comment on the language and what the poet is trying to convey. The first one is done for you.

Example	What it means	Comment on language
'The best of husbands are so hard to please'	Even if your husband is a really good one, they are still critical and difficult	A conversational tone, as though she is chatting to us about the problems with husbands
'No blustering husbands to create your fears'		
'No pangs of child birth to extort your tears'		
'No children's cries for to offend your ears'		
'Freed from all the cares'		

2 Explain in three sentences what the writer's attitude is towards marriage.

Developing your ideas

Activity 3

1 The speaker appears to be offering advice to a certain type of person. What evidence can you find from the poem about what sort of person this is?

2 Look closely at the following pairs of lines. For each, explain what you think it means. Then select one word or image that you find interesting. For example, for the first quotation you might say:

The poet uses the word 'crown'd' to highlight the happiness and peacefulness of the unmarried woman. It is an interesting image because a crown is something wonderful and precious.

A 'A virgin state is crown'd with much content,
It's always happy as it's innocent.'

B 'Supress wild nature if she dare rebel,
There's no such thing as leading apes in hell.'

C 'This in wifes careful faces you may spell,
Tho they desemble their misfortunes well.'

Activity 4

Developing a personal response

1 The poem was written in the seventeenth century. It contains a number of words that have a religious meaning. Make a list of them and think about why the poet has made these references. What link can you find between these images and male/female relationships? Explain your ideas in three or four sentences.

2 This poem protests against some of the unfairness and inequality in marriage in the seventeenth century. Women's situation today, and modern marriage, might be seen as very different. Which of the following comments do you agree with most?

Student A

'This poem has no real relevance to young women today. We can choose whether to have children, and marriages are equal.'

Student B

'This poem still has a lot of truth in it. Although partners are meant to be equal, in fact many men still want to be in control in a marriage.'

3 Compare the images of marriage and of single life in this poem with those in another poem. How does its message compare to Robert Herrick's, in 'To the Virgins, to Make Much of Time' (page 72)?

Peer/Self-assessment

MAKE THE GRADE

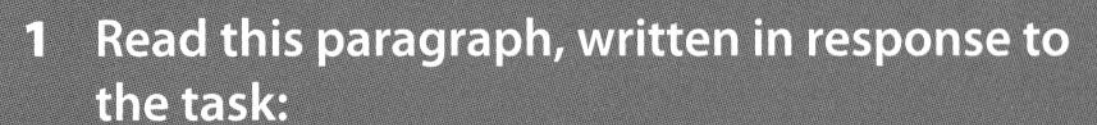

1 Read this paragraph, written in response to the task:
How does Philips present male/female relationships in 'A Married State'?

2 Write a paragraph giving your own response to the task. Use the same structure as the paragraph on the right.

3 Annotate your paragraph using the same notes as the paragraph on the right. If you have forgotten to include anything in your paragraph, add it in.

4 Which criteria in Assessment Objective 2 on page 134 have you demonstrated in your paragraph?

A clear point

Evidence to support the point

Philips presents marriage as something that should be avoided at all costs. Virgins are described as having:
'Few worldly crosses to distract your prayers.'
Here the image of the 'crosses' makes having a husband sound like a heavy burden that young women should avoid. There is also religious significance in the use of the 'cross' as an image, perhaps suggesting that women who marry risk becoming like martyrs.

An explanation of the effect of the quotation

How the language reflects the poet's point of view

Clear focus on the writer's choice of language

My learning objectives

- to explore the themes of the poem, including hypocrisy
- to develop my response to Thomas's poem
- to assess my work on Thomas's poem against the criteria in Assessment Objective 2 (page 134).

GradeStudio

Examiner tips

You can achieve a high grade if you:

- make detailed reference to the ideas, language and structure Thomas uses to convey the narrator's thoughts and viewpoint
- use well-chosen quotations from the poem to support your points on theme, content, language and structure
- explore comparisons and links that you can make between this poem about hypocrisy and other texts with similar themes.

Poem Glossary

Chapel: place of Christian worship
Deacon: assistant to the church minister
Staid: serious, unemotional
The Book: the Bible
Heifer: young cow
Kindled: alight
Deft: neat, skilful
Poise: calm, confident posture

His word was in my heart as a burning fire. (Jeremiah 20:9)

And suddenly there came a sound from heaven as of a rushing mighty wind, and it filled all the house where they were sitting... And they were all filled with the Holy Ghost. (Acts 2:2–4)

Chapel Deacon

by R. S. Thomas

First thoughts

Activity 1

1 Where is the narrator in the poem? What is he doing?

2 How would you expect a chapel deacon to think and act? Does Davies, the chapel deacon, think and act in this way? Is he being hypocritical?

Looking more closely

Activity 2

1 The narrator tells us that Davies has a 'crease' in his 'soul'. The word 'crease' can have different implications. We might iron a shirt to take the creases out, but iron a pair of trousers to put neat creases down the front!
   a What does the word suggest Davies has done to his soul, in getting 'ready ... For … chapel'?
   b Is this a positive or negative comment on Davies?

2 The narrator tells us that Davies can pray and scheme at once.
   a Why is he praying?
   b What is he scheming about?

3 The narrator describes Davies's 'lean cheeks' burning.
   a What two possible explanations does the narrator suggest?
   b What does each of these imply about Davies's character?

4 There is a faint breeze in the chapel, perhaps a metaphor for the presence of God.
   a The narrator says he 'roll[s] in it'. What does this suggest about the narrator?
   b The narrator says Davies maintains his 'deft poise'. What does this suggest about Davies?

Developing your ideas

Activity 3

1 The poem is full of contrasts.
   a Identify three examples of contrast in the poem.
   b How does the poet use them to influence your view of Davies?

2 Look at these quotations from the Bible:

And the Lord God formed man of the dust of the ground, and breathed into his nostrils the breath of life; and man became a living soul. (Genesis 2:7)

Then spake Jesus again unto them, saying, I am the light of the world: he that followeth me shall not walk in darkness, but shall have the light of life. (John 8:12)

a What do these images of light, fire and wind suggest to you?

b Think about how the poem uses this and other imagery. What do the words below add to your understanding of:

- Davies
- the narrator
- Thomas's view of the chapel and of God?

'crease' 'staid' 'frown' 'Sobers'
'sunlight 'pray' 'scheme' 'swift'
'Kindled' 'smouldering' 'faint'
'freshens' 'roll' 'poise'

Organise your thoughts in a table like this one:

The word ...	... is used to describe	It implies that ...
crease	Davies's soul	Davies has 'ironed' his soul so that it looks good: he is presenting himself as a much better person than he really is
staid	the chapel	

Activity 4

Developing a personal response

1 The poem is made up of a series of questions addressed directly to Davies, with one imperative (command) in which the narrator also tells us about himself.

a Think about the voice of the narrator as he asks these questions. What tone has Thomas created?

- Polite
- Angry
- Accusing
- Mystified
- Wondering
- Something else?

b Do the words 'Tell me, Davies ...' add to or change the poem's tone?

2 What might be the honest answers to the narrator's questions?

Peer/Self-assessment

1 You are going to explore this question:
How does Thomas present the hypocrisy in the character of Davies in 'Chapel Deacon'?
Choose two of the quotations below, and use them to write two paragraphs in which you:

- respond to the task
- comment on the effect of the writer's choice of imagery and language.

'Who put that crease in your soul,
Davies'

'Who taught you to pray
And scheme at once'

'is the burning
Of your lean cheeks because you sit
Too near that girl's smouldering gaze?'

'the faint breeze
From heaven freshens and I roll in it'

2 Which criteria in Assessment Objective 2 on page 134 have you demonstrated in your answer?

My learning objectives

- to explore the themes of the poem, including prejudice
- to develop my response to Thomas's poem
- to assess my work on Thomas's poem against the criteria in Assessment Objective 2 (page 134).

GradeStudio

Examiner tips

You can achieve a high grade if you:

- make detailed reference to the ideas, language and structure Thomas uses to convey the narrator's thoughts and create the poem's mood
- use well-chosen quotations from the poem to support your points on theme, content, language and structure
- explore comparisons and links that you can make between this poem about prejudice and other texts with similar themes.

Poem Glossary

Hunchback: a person whose back is hunched due to curvature of the spine
Bell at dark: a bell rung at dusk to signal the closing of the park

The Hunchback in the Park

by Dylan Thomas

Activity 1

First thoughts

1 Who is the hunchback in the park?

2 What do the other visitors think of him?

3 In stanza 3, Thomas tells us that the children call him 'mister'. What is their attitude towards him? Why do you think Thomas describes him as 'A solitary mister' in stanza 2?

Activity 2

Looking more closely

1 The hunchback is in the park from 'the opening of the garden lock' until the 'bell at dark'. What does this imply?

2 Look at Thomas's description of the hunchback's daily routine in stanza 2.
 a What does each of these details suggest?
 b Thomas compares the hunchback to a dog, sleeping in a kennel. Why does he point out that 'nobody chained him up'?

3 a Note down all the details Thomas uses to build up a picture of the park. How would you describe the park in one word?
 b Which elements of the park's life does the hunchback interact with? Which does he observe in isolation?

4 Thomas uses language and imagery to describe the hunchback as other than human. How many different examples can you find? What do they suggest?

Activity 3

Developing your ideas

1 In the final three stanzas, the narrator imagines what is going on in the hunchback's mind.
 a What does the hunchback create in his mind?
 b What does this suggest about his thoughts and feelings?
 c How does it reflect the narrator's view of him in the earlier stanzas?

2 In the final stanza, the narrator describes the end of the hunchback's day as though everything in the park is following him home to his kennel. Do you think Thomas is suggesting:
- these are the things he sees as he goes to his kennel
- everything and everyone are closing in and overwhelming him
- he carries all these images in his head and into his dreams
- something else?

3 Look at the statements and comments below. They are all about the punctuation and rhyme in the poem. Choose some of the statements and comments, find quotations from the poem to illustrate them, and explore their effect.

Statement	Comment
There is very little punctuation	This gives the impression of a series of isolated images, like a collage of unrelated snapshots, reflecting the hunchback's isolation
	This gives the poem an uninterrupted pace, flowing like time from morning till night, from the unlocking of the gate to the closing bell
There is no regular rhyme scheme	This creates a loose, disjointed structure, reflecting the different points of view Thomas uses
Thomas uses half-rhyme throughout the poem	This holds the poem together while giving its language a musical quality

Activity 4

Developing a personal response

1 How does the narrator's choice of language affect your response to:
 a the hunchback? b the truant boys?

2 Thomas creates his picture of the hunchback from three different points of view: his own as a child, the truant boys', and the hunchback's. How does each contribute to the overall picture?

3 The beginning and end of the poem describe the hunchback's lowly isolation. However, stanza 6 imagines something much more positive. How does it affect the poem's mood and your response to it?

Peer/Self-assessment

1 Answer true or false to the following statements:
I can find evidence for and comment on:
- **a** the way Thomas presents the hunchback
- **b** the way Thomas presents the truant boys
- **c** the way Thomas presents the park
- **d** the structure of the poem
- **e** the mood of the poem
- **f** my response to the poem.

2 If you answered 'false' to any statements, compare your ideas with a partner's.
Look again at the poem and your answers to the questions on these pages to help you.

3 What else can you say about this poem? Write a new set of true/false statements to assess a partner's understanding of 'The Hunchback in the Park'.

4 a Write two paragraphs responding to the task: **How does Dylan Thomas present prejudice in 'The Hunchback in the Park'?**

b Look at the grade descriptors on pages 148–155. What grade would you award your response?

My learning objectives

- to explore the themes of the poem, including prejudice
- to develop my response to Enright's poem
- to assess my work on Enright's poem against the criteria in Assessment Objective 2 (page 134).

GradeStudio

Examiner tips

You can achieve a high grade if you:

- make detailed reference to the ideas, language and structure Enright uses to convey the narrator's thoughts and viewpoint
- use well-chosen quotations from the poem to support your points on theme, content, language and structure
- explore comparisons and links that you can make between this poem about prejudice and other texts with similar themes.

Poem Glossary

Displaced person: refugee, person fleeing from home because of extreme danger
Pranked out: dressed in a showy way
Pawky: cunning, sly
Brawny: strong, muscular
Florid: flamboyant
Fair: beautiful

Displaced Person Looks at a Cage-bird

by D. J. Enright

Activity 1

First thoughts

1. a There are two characters in this poem. Who are they?
   b What is your first reaction to them? What is each a victim of, and how does each one's situation make you feel?
2. How does the narrator suggest that these two characters could be made more similar? What point might the narrator be making here?

Activity 2

Looking more closely

1. a There is only one difference between lines 1 and 7 of the poem. What is it? What does it suggest?
   b Why has the narrator repeated himself in these lines?
   c The narrator writes about 'where I stay'. Why do you think he chooses the word 'stay' rather than 'live'? The title of the poem may give you a clue.
2. In stanza 2 the narrator describes the cage-bird.
   a Only one word clearly identifies the bird. What is it?
   b What do all the other describing words suggest to you?
   c Why do you think the narrator has chosen to do this?
3. Look at the first lines of the third and fourth stanzas. What is the effect of this repetition?
4. In his poem 'Composed Upon Westminster Bridge', William Wordsworth writes about London and says: 'Earth has not anything to show more fair'.
   a How has the narrator borrowed this line?
   b What does it suggest?
   c What do you think the narrator means by the word 'fair' here? See the Glossary opposite. Is he using it in two senses?

Activity 3

Developing your ideas

1. In lines 3–6, the narrator gives an extended description of the canary, listing reasons why he dislikes it.
   a Why has he chosen to write lists?
   b Is this an accurate description of a canary? Why is he describing it in this way?

2 In lines 10–11 the narrator again gives a list of reasons for disliking the canary.
   a In what ways does this list differ from the one in lines 3–6? Think about what he criticises the bird for – and the language he uses to do it.
   b The narrator describes the bird as:
   'rent-free' 'over-fed' 'Feather-bedded'
   'pensioned' 'free from wear and tear'
   Write a sentence or two commenting on the meaning and implications of each.

3 What does the narrator's attitude to the bird suggest about his feelings as a displaced person?

Developing a personal response

Activity 4

1 Other than in the title, the narrator does not mention the bird's cage.
   a What might the cage symbolise?
   b Why do you think the poet chooses *not* to refer to it?

2 Re-read the final stanza.
   a Why might the bird help him write better poetry if it were dead?
   b In the last three words of the poem, the narrator connects his own experience with the bird's. Does the narrator wish he were dead?

3 Do you think the narrator is describing the bird as if it were human, using personification? Or could the narrator be describing a person as if he were a bird, using zoomorphism? Explain your answer, using quotations from the poem as evidence.

4 How do you think Enright wants us to respond to the narrator as a displaced person?

Peer/Self-assessment

MAKE THE GRADE MAKE THE GRADE

1 Answer true or false to the following statements.
   I can find evidence for and comment on:
   a the way Enright presents the canary
   b the way Enright presents the displaced person's thoughts and feelings
   c Enright's use of language in the poem
   d the poet's point of view on the suffering of the displaced person in the poem
   e my response to the poem.

2 If you answered 'false' to any statements, compare your ideas with a partner's.
   Look again at the poem and your answers to the questions on these pages to help you.

3 What else can you say about this poem? Write a new set of true/false statements to assess a partner's understanding of 'Displaced Person looks at a Cage-bird'.

4 a Write two paragraphs responding to the task:
   How does Enright present the effects of prejudice on a person in 'Displaced Person Looks at a Cage-bird'?
   b Look at the grade descriptors on pages 148–155. What grade would you award your response?

Base Details

by Siegfried Sassoon

My learning objectives

- to explore the themes of the poem, including hypocrisy
- to develop my response to Sassoon's poem
- to assess my work on Sassoon's poem against the criteria in Assessment Objective 2 (page 134).

GradeStudio

MAKE THE GRADE

Examiner tips

You can achieve a high grade if you:

- make detailed reference to the language and structure Sassoon uses to convey the narrator's thoughts and viewpoint, and to create the poem's mood
- use well-chosen quotations from the poem to support your points on theme, content, language and structure
- explore comparisons and links that you can make between this poem about hypocrisy and other texts with similar themes.

Poem Glossary

The line: the line to the battle front
Petulant: annoyed, bad-tempered
Scrap: slang term for a battle

Activity 1

First thoughts

'Base Details' was written in 1917–18 during the First World War. Sassoon's early poetry – including 'Base Details' – was inspired by his experiences as a soldier fighting in France.

1 The poem describes army majors safely stationed at their base and, in the end, dying in their beds.
  a What is the cause of their death? When will this happen?
  b How will the regular soldiers die? When will this happen?

2 'Base' has several meanings. Two of them are on the right:
  a What does the title of the poem refer to?
  b What does it suggest?

- a camp or building away from the battlefield, from which military operations are planned
- dishonourable, selfish, cowardly

Activity 2

Looking more closely

1 a Identify the words and phrases Sassoon chooses to describe the army majors, and the ones he uses to describe regular soldiers.
  b Write a sentence or two explaining what each of these words and phrases suggests about the majors and their soldiers. You could record your responses in a table like this:

	Words/phrases	This suggests
Describing the majors	fierce	The soldiers are afraid of them
	short of breath	Fat, unfit
	toddle	
Describing the soldiers	glum	

  c What do you notice about the number of words and phrases used to describe the majors, and the number used to describe the soldiers?
  d How does this reflect the majors' attitude?

2 In the third line, Sassoon describes the regular soldiers as 'glum heroes'.
 a Do you expect heroes to be glum, or something different?
 b Do you think these men are heroes? Write two sentences arguing they are, then two that they are not.

3 Look at the dialogue in lines 6–8. What does it suggest about the majors' attitudes towards:
 a people and their families b war, soldiers and their death?

Activity 3

Developing your ideas

1 How would you describe the mood of the poem:
 • angry • bitter • sarcastic • something else?
 Think of at least one other word.

2 The poet uses alliteration. For example:
 'You'd see me with my puffy petulant face'
 a Find at least one other example of alliteration.
 b How does this add to the tone the poet has created?
 c Pick three examples of words or language features that you feel contribute most to the poem's tone.

3 a The rhyme scheme follows a specific pattern for the first eight lines. What is it?
 b How does it change in the last two lines? What effect does this create?
 c How does the dash in the final line add to this effect?

Activity 4

Developing a personal response

1 The poet's attitude to the majors seems very damning. Is any other interpretation of this poem possible?

2 The poem begins 'If I were ...'. Do you think this suggests:
 • if the poet were a major, he would behave in this way
 • he does not blame them for their behaviour
 • this is how all majors behave
 • something else?

Peer/Self-assessment

1 Read this paragraph, written in response to the task:
 How does Sassoon present hypocritical attitudes to war in 'Base Details'?
2 Write a paragraph giving your own response to the task. Use the same structure as the paragraph on the right.
3 Annotate your paragraph using the same notes as the paragraph on the right. If you have forgotten to include anything in your paragraph, add it in.
4 Which criteria in Assessment Objective 2 on page 134 have you demonstrated in your paragraph?

Evidence to support the point

A clear point

Sassoon describes a casual attitude to war: 'Yes, we've lost heavily in this last scrap.' The major does not acknowledge the suffering and death toll which Sassoon highlights earlier in the poem; 'lost heavily' makes it sound like a game of cricket or rugby, while 'scrap' suggests a playground fight, not a war in which millions of lives were lost. This implies that the major is unconcerned by the carnage, and is behaving like a foolish child.

An explanation of the effect of the quotation

How language reflects the poet's point of view

Close focus on particular word choice

My learning objectives

- to explore the themes of the poem, including prejudice and hypocrisy
- to develop my response to Pugh's poem
- to assess my work on Pugh's poem against the criteria in Assessment Objective 2 (page 134).

The Capon Clerk

by Sheenagh Pugh

First thoughts

Activity 1

1. Who is the narrator of the poem? Look at the full title.
2. Look closely at the poem's last stanza. What does it suggest about people who write love poetry?
3. Look at the Glossary on the next page. How does the poem's title add to your understanding of the narrator's point of view? What is the narrator attacking?

Looking more closely

Activity 2

1. In stanza 2 the narrator writes about the poet of love's suffering.
   a. Why is he suffering?
   b. Why does he 'pride' himself on this suffering?
2. In stanza 3, the narrator contrasts starving and feeding.
   a. What is she suggesting?
   b. Who does the poet of love blame for his starvation?
3. Look at stanza 4. Who does the narrator blame for the poet of love's starvation? Why – according to the narrator – does he behave in this way?
4. Look at stanza 5. How does the poet of love want other men to react to his sad poetry?
5. In stanzas 6 and 7, the narrator sums up a number of reasons why, she believes, the poet of love writes his poetry.
   a. What are they?
   b. One reason the narrator suggests is that he 'loves the scansion' of her name. Why might this be?

Developing your ideas

Activity 3

1. Throughout the poem, the narrator describes the poet of love's thoughts, actions and motives.
   a. What does he like to do to help him write his love poetry? Make a list of quotations from the poem.
   b. What does each of the quotations you have selected tell you about the poet of love's character?
   c. Choose one word from each quotation that tells you most about the poet of love's character. What does it suggest? For example:

Suggests it is not real pain – it is like make-up

'He loves to paint his face with pain'

suggests he enjoys feeling sorry for himself and likes others to feel sorry for him too.

2 Of all the insults and complaints the narrator uses against the poet of love, the poem's title is, perhaps, the worst.

a What does the word 'capon' suggest about the poet of love? You could record your thoughts on a mind map:

Castrated, not a 'real man'

b In stanza 1, the narrator says that the poet of love 'crows'. How many different meanings can you think of for this word? What does each suggest about the poet and his voice?

c What does the word 'clerk' suggest about the poet of love's writing?

3 The poem's subtitle – *Complaint of a Troubadour's Lady* – suggests its tone.

a Pick out at least five words that show how strongly the narrator presents her complaint.

b How would you sum up the tone of the poem?

Activity 4

Developing a personal response

1 In stanza 1, the narrator addresses someone by the name 'sir'.

a Who is she talking to?

b What does this suggest the purpose of the poem might be?

2 Looking at the poem as a whole, what events might have prompted the narrator to write her complaint?

3 Do you think the narrator is justified in her complaint? Choose evidence from the poem to support your response.

GradeStudio

Examiner tips

You can achieve a high grade if you:

- make detailed reference to the language and structure Pugh uses to convey the narrator's thoughts and viewpoint
- use well-chosen quotations from the poem to support your points on theme, content, language and structure
- explore comparisons and links that you can make between this poem about hypocrisy and prejudice and other texts with similar themes.

Poem Glossary

Capon: castrated male chicken
Clerk: office worker who writes reports, keeps accounts, etc.
Troubadour: wandering minstrel – singer and composer of songs
Grace: kindness, generosity
Scansion: rhythm or stress pattern in poetry

Peer/Self-assessment

1 You are going to explore this question:
How does Pugh present the hypocrisy of the poet of love in 'The Capon Clerk'?
Choose two of the quotations below, and use them to write two paragraphs in which you:

- respond to the task
- comment on the effect of the writer's choice of language.

'a man who hotly pleads for grace
and cools upon the offer.'

'He loves to paint his face with pain
and pose his shabby figure
where men may toss him sympathy'

'The liar, he would not enter in
if I sent an invitation.'

'he loves the scansion of my name,
but sure he loves not me, sir.'

2 Which criteria in Assessment Objective 2 on page 134 have you demonstrated in your answer?

You Will Be Hearing From Us Shortly

by U. A. Fanthorpe

My learning objectives

- to explore the themes of the poem, including prejudice
- to develop my response to Fanthorpe's poem
- to assess my work on Fanthorpe's poem against the criteria in Assessment Objective 2 (page 134).

GradeStudio

Examiner tips

You can achieve a high grade if you:

- make detailed reference to the ideas, language and structure Fanthorpe uses to convey the narrator's thoughts and create the poem's mood
- use well-chosen quotations from the poem to support your points on theme, content, language and structure
- explore comparisons and links that you can make between this poem about prejudice and other texts with similar themes.

Poem Glossary

Perpetuate: cause to continue

Activity 1

First thoughts

The poem recounts one side of a conversation between an interviewer and a job applicant.

1. What are your first impressions of:
   - the interviewer
   - the job applicant
   - the interviewer's attitude to the job applicant?
2. Do you think the job applicant will be successful? Write a sentence or two explaining your answer.

Activity 2

Looking more closely

1. In stanza 1, the interviewer asks about the job applicant's 'qualities'. What do you think he or she means?
2. In stanza 2, the interviewer comments on the job applicant's qualifications. What is wrong with them?
3. Which areas does the interviewer concentrate on in the remaining stanzas? What is the problem with each one? Match the stanza to the area of questioning and the problem. Note that in one area of questioning, the problem is not explained.

Stanza	Area of questioning	The problem
3	Being born	'the need for a candidate with precisely The right degree of immaturity.'
4	Accent	'And how Much of a handicap is that to you'
5	Looks	'to perpetuate what had better Not have happened at all.'
6	Family	'Might they, Perhaps, find your appearance Disturbing?'
7	Age	

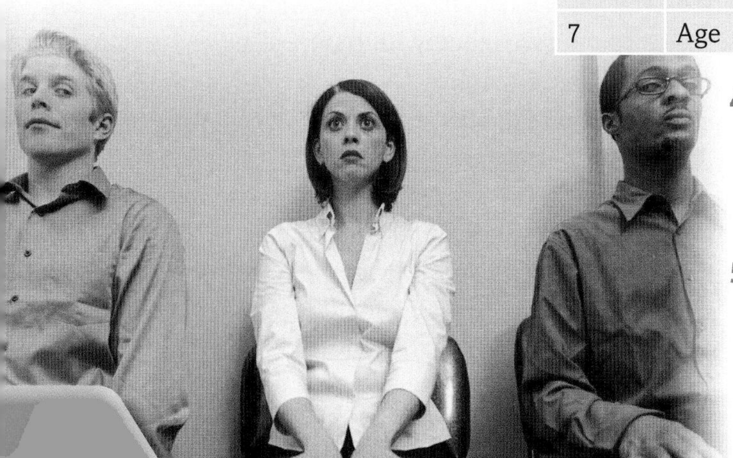

4. Look at line 38, near the end of the poem: 'Yes. Pity.'
   a. What does the interviewer think is a pity?
   b. What does this suggest about his or her opinion of this job applicant?
5. Write a list of the qualities this interviewer is looking for. What kind of job or company do you think the interview is for?

Activity 3

Developing your ideas

1 Look at these examples of the language the interviewer uses:
'adequate' 'demands' 'this position' 'qualities' 'Let us consider'
   a How would you describe this kind of language?
      - formal
      - sophisticated
      - superior
      - arrogant
      - pompous?
   b Is this choice of language appropriate to the situation in which it is being used?
   c What does it suggest about the interviewer?

2 The voice of the job applicant does not appear in the poem at all. Why do you think this might be?
   - To disempower the job applicant and show he or she is much less important than the interviewer?
   - Because the job applicant's answers are so irrelevant, they are not even worth writing down?
   - Because the poem is about the interviewer and his or her prejudice, not the job applicant?
   - So readers can put themselves in the job applicant's place?
   - All of the above?
   - Something else?

3 Some of interviewer's words are set to the right-hand side of the page. Why do you think this is?

4 What do you think the job applicant says in reply to all these questions? Write down what the job applicant might say in the gaps Fanthorpe has left in the poem.

Activity 4

Developing a personal response

1 What does this poem suggest about:
   - job interviews
   - interviewers
   - job applicants?

2 You will probably agree that this is an angry poem. Do you also find it funny? How has Fanthorpe used humour to influence your response to the poem?

Peer/Self-assessment

1 You are going to explore this question:
How does Fanthorpe explore prejudice in 'You Will Be Hearing From Us Shortly'?
Choose three of the quotations below, and use them to write three paragraphs in which you:
- respond to the task
- comment on the effect of the writer's choice of language.

'Where were you educated?
And how
Much of a handicap is that to you'

'Not, we must admit, precisely what
We had in mind.'

'the need for a candidate with precisely
The right degree of immaturity'

'The usual dubious
Desire to perpetuate what had better
Not have happened at all.'

'Might they,
Perhaps, find your appearance
Disturbing?'

'And you were born – ?
Yes. Pity.'

2 Which criteria in Assessment Objective 2 on page 134 have you demonstrated in your answer?

Refugee Blues

by W. H. Auden

First thoughts

Activity 1

In 'Refugee Blues' – written in 1939, just before the outbreak of the Second World War – Auden takes on the voice of one of thousands of German Jews fleeing to Europe and America from Hitler's persecution.

1. Blues has its origins in the music of Afro-American slaves. Can you see any similarities between their situation and the situation of the people in the poem?
2. Blues music is often improvised (made up as the musician goes along), but the notes follow regular patterns, and phrases are repeated as a chorus. How does the poem reflect this?
3. The poem explores the problems the narrator encounters, mostly caused by hypocrisy and prejudice. List them. For example, the narrator:
   - has nowhere to live

Looking more closely

Activity 2

1. The third line of every stanza gives clues about who the narrator is talking to.
   a What are the clues? b Who is it?
   c What image does this create in your mind?
   d How does it affect your response to the poem?
2. In stanza 2, the narrator talks of his or her country, and says that 'we thought it fair'. The word 'fair' has a number of meanings:
   - following the rules; just and honest
   - beautiful
   - not good, not bad, just average

   a Which of these meanings do you think Auden intends here?
   b Which meaning is given greater impact by the stanza's last line?
3. Auden uses images of nature throughout.
   a What effects do these create?
   b How does their presentation compare with the presentation of human life?
4. Auden describes 'a poodle in a jacket' and 'a door opened and a cat let in'.
   a What do you think these two symbols represent?
   b What privileges do the dog and cat have which are denied to German Jews?

My learning objectives

- to explore the themes of the poem, including prejudice
- to develop my response to Auden's poem
- to assess my work on Auden's poem against the criteria in Assessment Objective 2 (page 134).

GradeStudio

MAKE THE GRADE

Examiner tips

You can achieve a high grade if you:

- make detailed reference to the language and structure Auden uses to convey the narrator's thoughts and viewpoint
- use well-chosen quotations from the poem to support your points on theme, content, language and structure
- explore comparisons and links that you can make between this poem about prejudice and other texts with similar themes.

Poem Glossary

Refugee: person fleeing from home because of extreme danger
Blues: music expressing sadness, originally developed by black Americans at the end of the nineteenth century
Consul: official appointed by a government to help its citizens in a foreign country

Activity 3

Developing your ideas

1 Several stanzas begin with a verb, with its subject left out, so rather than writing 'I went to a committee', Auden writes 'Went to a committee'. What is the effect of this informal style?

2 Many of the poem's stanzas use contrast to make their point. For example:
In stanza 1, Auden contrasts those who are 'living in mansions' with those 'living in holes'. This emphasises a great divide in society: some are privileged while others are forced to live like animals.
Identify at least three further examples of contrast. Write a sentence or two explaining the effect of each.

3 In stanza 11, Auden describes a dream about a building.
   a What do you think he is suggesting by describing its thousand floors, doors and windows?
   b Why has he chosen to repeat the number 'a thousand' three times?
   c How does this stanza sum up the narrator's situation?

4 Look closely at the image in the last stanza. The poet describes:
   - a great plain
   - snow
   - ten thousand soldiers
   - you and me.

   What does each of these elements contribute to the image?

Activity 4

Developing a personal response

Look at this range of different responses to the task:

How does Auden present the way the narrator faces hypocrisy and prejudice in 'Refugee Blues'?

- The narrator's personal freedom and dignity are being destroyed, slowly but surely.
- The poet builds our sympathy every time the narrator addresses his or her partner.
- Our sympathy reaches a peak in the final stanza as they face almost certain death.
- The poet uses images from nature throughout the poem.

Turn each of these responses into point-evidence-explanation paragraphs by:

- finding evidence for each response
- adding a sentence or two explaining how and why your evidence supports each response.

Peer/Self-assessment

1 **Look at your answer to Activity 4 above, and at the grade descriptors on pages 148–155. What grade would you award your answer?**
2 **What could you change or add to improve your response? Use the grade descriptors to identify the two things most likely to improve your grade.**
3 **Redraft your answer, trying to make those changes.**
4 **Look again at the grade descriptors. Have you improved your grade?**

In Church

by Thomas Hardy

My learning objectives

- to explore the themes of the poem, including hypocrisy
- to develop my response to Hardy's poem
- to assess my work on Hardy's poem against the criteria in Assessment Objective 2 (page 134).

GradeStudio

Examiner tips

You can achieve a high grade if you:

- make detailed reference to the language and structure Hardy uses to convey the narrator's thoughts and viewpoint
- use well-chosen quotations from the poem to support your points on theme, content, language and structure
- explore comparisons and links that you can make between this poem about hypocrisy and other texts with similar themes.

Poem Glossary

Pervades: spreads through every part
Vestry: side room off a church, often used for preparation and storage
Gloss: deliberately misleading appearance
Guile: craftiness, trickery
Glass: mirror

First thoughts

Activity 1

1. The poem is structured in two stanzas. Where does the action described in each stanza take place?
2. 'In Church' is a narrative poem: it tells a story. Summarise the story in one or two sentences. What does it suggest about the preacher's real attitudes, in contrast to what they appear to be?

Looking more closely

Activity 2

1. Look at these verbs taken from stanza 1:
   'thrills' 'chokes' 'bows' 'bends' 'pervades' 'glides'
   a Divide them into:
   - words chosen to describe the preacher's actions
   - words chosen to describe their effect on the congregation.

   b What do these language choices – individually and collectively – suggest about the preacher and his congregation?
2. The congregation is referred to as 'Each listener' and the 'crowded aisles'. What does each of these language choices suggest about the congregation and the preacher?
3. The title of the poem and its first line immediately tell us this is about a preacher in church. Without these clues, what other job might you assume this man did? Write a sentence or two explaining your answer, supported by at least one quotation.
4. **a** In stanza 2, Hardy describes the pupil's feelings towards the preacher. Which word in these lines sums up her feelings?
   b How does Hardy describe the pupil's reaction once she has seen him in the vestry?
   c Why do you think this is?
5. Now look at Hardy's choice of language to describe the preacher in the vestry:
   'satisfied smile' 're-enact' 'gesture'
   'deft dumb-show'
   What does each of these language choices suggest – individually and collectively – about the preacher?

Developing your ideas

Activity 3

1 Think about the preacher's actions and his audience, and the different situations in stanza 1 and stanza 2. In what ways are they different? In what ways are they similar? How does stanza 2 'mirror' the first?

2 Hardy uses alliteration throughout the poem.
  a Identify examples – and note what he is describing.
  b Why has Hardy chosen to use alliteration to describe these actions and reactions?

Developing a personal response

Activity 4

1 Imagine you are the pupil in the poem.
  a How would you react to seeing the preacher in this situation?
  b How have the poet's choices created or influenced your response?

2 Look at these two responses to the poem:

Student A:

It seems that the preacher enjoys manipulating his congregation. His 'satisfied smile' in the 'vestry-glass' suggests a vanity that a preacher should not have. The image of him gazing adoringly at himself, smug in his own cleverness, is an almost sinister picture of a man who should be anything but sinister.

Student B:

At first glance, the poem seems to be condemning the preacher. But it is his skill in preaching that has filled the 'crowded aisles', and made the young girl in the poem see him as her 'idol'. A preacher should be charismatic and inspire the congregation. This preacher is clearly very successful.

  a What is your response to the character of the preacher? Write at least two paragraphs supporting your response, with quotations and detailed comments on Hardy's choice of language.
  b Do you think it was Hardy's intention to create this response in the reader? Write a sentence or two explaining your answer.

Peer/Self-assessment

1 Look again at the paragraphs you wrote in response to question 2a in Activity 4 above. You are now going to explore this question:
What is your response to the hypocrisy shown by the preacher in 'In Church'?
Choose three quotations from the poem and use them to write three paragraphs in which you:
- respond to the task
- comment on the effect of the writer's choice of language.

2 Look at the grade descriptors on pages 148–155. What grade would you award your response?

3 What could you change or add to improve your response? Use the grade descriptors to identify the two things most likely to improve your grade.

4 Redraft your answer, trying to make those changes.

5 Look again at the grade descriptors. Have you improved your grade?

Dulce et Decorum Est

by Wilfred Owen

My learning objectives

- to explore the themes of the poem, including conflict
- to develop my response to Owen's poem
- to assess my work on Owen's poem against the criteria in Assessment Objective 2 (page 134).

GradeStudio

Examiner tips

You can achieve a high grade if you:

- make detailed reference to the language and structure Owen uses to convey the narrator's thoughts and viewpoint
- use well-chosen quotations from the poem to support your points on theme, content, language and structure
- explore comparisons and links that you can make between this war poem and other texts with similar themes.

Poem Glossary

Ecstasy: frenzy
Lime: chemical that can burn the skin; used to speed the decomposition of a buried corpse
Ardent: intensely enthusiastic
Dulce et decorum est pro patria mori: how sweet and fitting it is to die for one's country

First thoughts

Activity 1

The poem was written in 1917, during the First World War, in which Wilfred Owen served as a soldier.

1 Write down the sequence of events described in the poem.

2 a What are your first impressions of the way Owen presents war? Choose three words or phrases as examples.
b What does this suggest about Owen's choice of title?

Looking more closely

Activity 2

1 a Re-read stanza 1. Write down the words and phrases that describe the soldiers.
b Pick the three words or phrases that tell you most about the soldiers. What does each suggest to you?

2 a Re-read stanza 2. How does Owen use language, punctuation and point of view to change the mood and focus of the poem here?
b How are the verbs in this stanza both similar to and different from the verbs in stanza 1?

3 In stanza 2, Owen describes the 'green light'. What has happened?

4 Re-read stanza 3. The dying man is described as 'guttering'. Look at these dictionary definitions of the word:

- flowing, streaming down
- burning unsteadily, flicker so as to be almost extinguished

Which of these meanings is Owen using? What effect does he create?

5 a Re-read the final stanza. Write down all the words and phrases Owen uses to describe the dying man.
b Pick the three words or phrases that tell you most. What does each suggest to you?

Activity 3

Developing your ideas

1 Look carefully at the structure of the poem. In which stanza does Owen use these techniques to create which effects?

Stanza	Technique	Effect
1	The past tense	Puts readers in the soldiers' shoes, insisting that they consider how they would feel if they witnessed such events, and must re-think their views on war
2	Direct address to the reader – 'you', 'My friend'	Emphasises the stark horror of the event – and the horrific effect on the narrator
3	Many present participles (-ing verbs)	Suggests a story being told
4	A much shorter stanza	Creates a feeling of frantic action happening in front of us

2 The final line is much shorter than the others. What effect is created?

3 Much of the poem's vocabulary is graphic and disturbing. Choose three examples and show how the poet uses them.

4 Look at the underlined words in each of these examples of Owen's language choices. What does each suggest to you?

A 'coughing like <u>hags</u>'
B 'An <u>ecstasy</u> of fumbling'
C 'In all my dreams, before my <u>helpless</u> sight'
D '<u>children</u> ardent for some desperate glory'

Activity 4

Developing a personal response

1 What do you think is Owen's intention in writing this poem?

2 How do each of the following features contribute to that intention?

- The story Owen has chosen to tell.
- The graphic language.
- The frequent use of simile.
- The direct address to the audience.
- The title.

Peer/Self-assessment

1 You are going to explore this question:
How does Owen present war in 'Dulce et Decorum Est'?
Choose three of the quotations below, and use them to write three paragraphs in which you:
- respond to the task
- comment on the effect of the writer's choice of language.

'Bent double, like old beggars under sacks,
Knock-kneed, coughing like hags, we cursed through sludge'

'Gas! GAS! Quick, boys! – An ecstasy of fumbling,
Fitting the clumsy helmets just in time'

'In all my dreams, before my helpless sight,
He plunges at me, guttering, choking, drowning.'

'If you could hear, at every jolt, the blood
Come gargling from the froth-corrupted lungs'

'My friend, you would not tell with such high zest
To children ardent for some desperate glory,
The old Lie'

2 Which criteria in Assessment Objective 2 on page 134 have you demonstrated in your answer?

My learning objectives

- to explore the themes of the poem, including conflict
- to develop my response to Thomas's poem
- to assess my work on Thomas's poem against the criteria in Assessment Objective 2 (page 134).

GradeStudio

MAKE THE GRADE MAKE THE GRADE

Examiner tips

You can achieve a high grade if you:

- make detailed reference to the language and structure Thomas uses to convey the narrator's thoughts and ideas
- use well-chosen quotations from the poem to support your points on theme, content, language and structure
- explore comparisons and links that you can make between this war poem and other texts with similar themes.

Poem Glossary

Zion: Jerusalem, used symbolically for the Promised Land or Heaven
Sackcloth: a rough cloth worn to show penitence or mourning
Stations: the 14 stations of the cross are stages in Jesus Christ's journey to crucifixion
Elegy: poem written in memory of someone who has died

A Refusal to Mourn the Death, by Fire, of a Child in London

by Dylan Thomas

Activity 1

First thoughts

Written in 1945 during the Second World War, this poem explains why Thomas will not mourn the death of a child killed in a London bombing raid.

1 Look for any language that indicates the poet's emotional reaction to the death. How many examples can you find? Why do you think this is?

2 Many poems have been written to mourn a person's death. Why do you think Thomas is refusing to mourn this death? Give evidence from the poem.

Activity 2

Looking more closely

1 Thomas describes darkness as
'mankind making
Bird beast and flower
Fathering and all humbling darkness'
a What do you think he is referring to?
b Why is he referring to it as 'darkness'?

2 Thomas says he will mourn when
'the last light breaking
And the still hour
Is come'
What do you think he means?

3 Finally, in line 13, Thomas refers to 'the child's death'. Look closely at this line. Why does Thomas choose 'majesty' and 'burning' to describe the child's death?

4 The child is not named and Thomas makes no reference to her family. Why do you think he describes her as 'London's daughter'?

5 Thomas goes on to describe the child's buried body as:
'Robed in the long friends,
The grains beyond age, the dark veins of her mother,
Secret by the unmourning water
Of the riding Thames.'
a To what might the three images in the first two lines refer?
b Why do you think he describes the water as 'unmourning'?
c How does this reflect Thomas's own attitude to the death?

6 Re-read the first and last lines of the final stanza. Do you think Thomas is suggesting that:
- the first time we experience the death of someone close is the worst
- if only one person dies in war, it is too many; further deaths cannot make it worse
- death is a part of life, and we should not mourn
- something else?

Developing your ideas

Activity 3

Look at this selection of language from the poem:
'Bird beast and flower' 'Fathering' 'darkness' 'the last light'
'the still hour' 'the sea' 'the water bead' 'the ear of corn'
'the child's death' 'murder' 'blaspheme' 'the stations of the breath'
'the first dead' 'grains' 'veins' 'water'
Sort these examples of Thomas's vocabulary into groups of your own choosing. Give each group a title. What seems important to Thomas in his choice of language?

Developing a personal response

Activity 4

1 Thousands of civilians died in the Second World War. Why do you think the death of the child prompted Thomas to write this poem?

2 Look at these phrases from the poem:
'Never' 'I must' 'I shall not' 'there is no other'
How would you describe the tone Thomas uses in the poem? Is it:
- anger
- certainty
- defiance
- suppressed emotion
- something else?

Peer/Self-assessment

1 **You are going to explore this question:**
How does Thomas present his thoughts and feelings about human conflict in 'A Refusal to Mourn ...'?
Choose three of the quotations below, and use them to write three paragraphs in which you:
- **respond to the task**
- **comment on the effect of the writer's choice of language.**

'Never until the mankind making
Bird beast and flower
Fathering and all humbling darkness'

'The majesty and burning of the child's death.'

'I shall not murder
The mankind of her going with a grave truth'

'Deep with the first dead lies London's daughter,
Robed in the long friends,
The grains beyond age, the dark veins of her mother'

'After the first death, there is no other.'

2 **Which criteria in Assessment Objective 2 on page 134 have you demonstrated in your answer?**

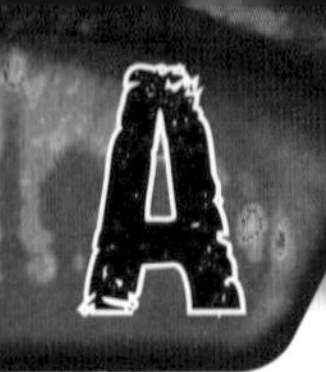

My learning objectives

- to explore the themes of the poem, including conflict
- to develop my response to Brooke's poem
- to assess my work on Brooke's poem against the criteria in Assessment Objective 2 (page 134).

GradeStudio

Examiner tips

MAKE THE GRADE

You can achieve a high grade if you:

- make detailed reference to the language and structure Brooke uses to convey the narrator's thoughts
- use well-chosen quotations from the poem to support your points on theme, content, language and structure
- explore comparisons and links that you can make between this war poem and other texts with similar themes.

The Soldier

by Rupert Brooke

Activity 1

First thoughts

'The Soldier' was written in 1914, at the outbreak of the First World War.

1 The poem is written in the first person. Who is speaking?

2 Where do you think the narrator might be as he writes?

3 What general attitudes towards war does the poem express?

Activity 2

Looking more closely

1 If he dies, where does the narrator expect to be buried?

2 Once buried, how does the narrator imagine that his body will make 'some corner of a foreign field ... for ever England'?

3 What does the narrator believe that England has given him?

4 The narrator describes his body as 'A body of England's'. What does this phrase suggest to you?

5 After death, the narrator imagines himself becoming 'A pulse in the eternal mind'. What is he suggesting?

6 In the last three lines of the poem, the narrator describes what his 'pulse in the eternal mind' will give back. Now compare this with what England has given him, described in stanza 1. What does this suggest?

7 Look at the last few words of the poem: 'under an English heaven'.
   a What is the narrator's view of heaven?
   b What is the narrator's view of England?

Activity 3

Developing your ideas

1 Look closely at the vocabulary Brooke has chosen to use.
   a Giving as many examples as you can, add words and phrases from the poem to your copy of the table below:

Language of war	Language of peace
die	rich earth flowers to love

   b What do you notice? What does this suggest?

2 a What do we learn from the poem about the soldier's views on England?
   b What else do we learn about the soldier himself?
   c Compare your answers to (a) and (b). What does this suggest about the poet's intentions in writing 'The Soldier'?

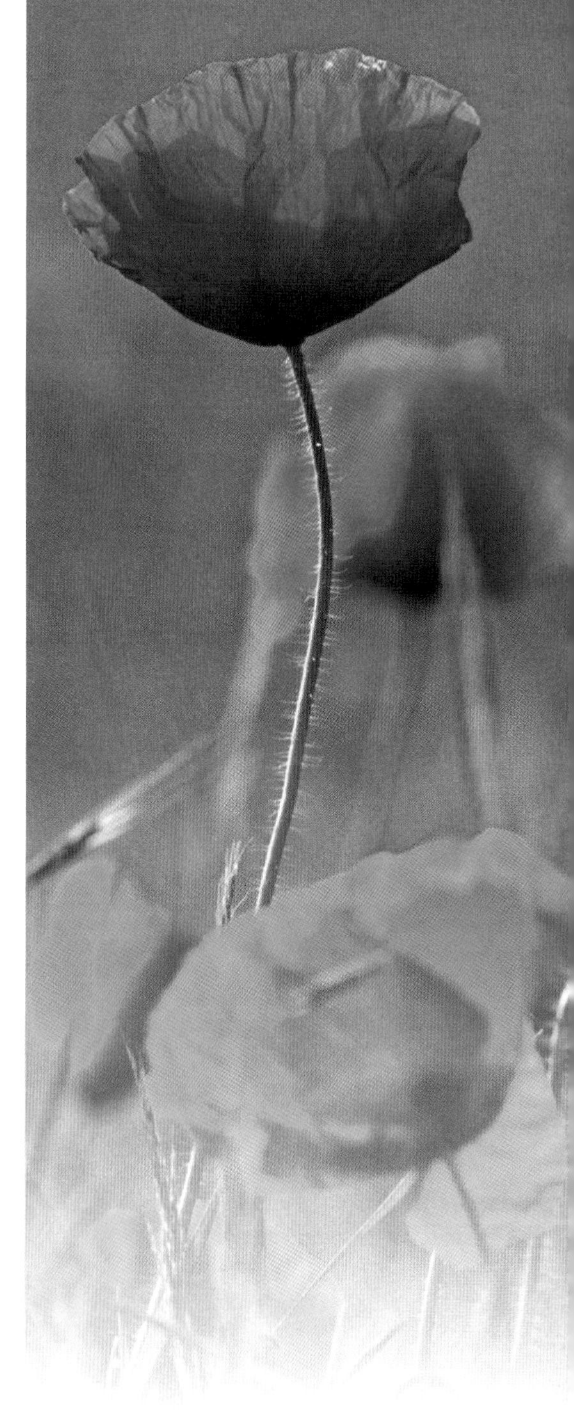

3 Compare the first line of stanza 1 with the first line of stanza 2.
   a One verb appears in both lines. Who is the narrator addressing?
   b What effect do you think is intended?

4 Now compare the second lines of the two stanzas. How has the focus of the poem changed from the first to the second?

5 a Think of three other possible titles for the poem and explain why you have chosen them.
   b Why do you think Brooke chose 'The Soldier' as his title?

Developing a personal response

Activity 4

1 What clues are there in the poem that it was written at the start of the First World War?

2 Look at this range of different responses to the task:
   How does Rupert Brooke present the narrator's view of war in 'The Soldier'?
   - The narrator strongly believes it is a soldier's duty to fight for his country.
   - The narrator expresses the view that, considering everything our country has given us, we should be prepared to give everything we have when our country needs us – even our lives.
   - The narrator ignores the brutality of war, focusing on the nobility of giving one's life for one's country.
   - The narrator is encouraging people to fight for their country with unthinking patriotism and arrogant nationalism.
   - The poem is not about war, it is about England.

   Turn three of these responses into point-evidence-explanation paragraphs by:
   - finding evidence for each response
   - adding a sentence or two explaining how and why your evidence supports each response.

Peer/Self-assessment

1 **Look at your answer to question 2 in Activity 4 above, and at the grade descriptors on pages 148–155. What grade would you award your answer?**
2 **What could you change or add to improve your response? Use the grade descriptors to identify the two things most likely to improve your grade.**
3 **Redraft your answer, trying to make those changes.**
4 **Look again at the grade descriptors. Have you improved your grade?**

My learning objectives

- to explore the themes of the poem, including conflict
- to develop my response to Gibson's poem
- to assess my work on Gibson's poem against the criteria in Assessment Objective 2 (page 134).

GradeStudio

Examiner tips

You can achieve a high grade if you:

- make detailed reference to the language and structure Gibson uses to convey the narrator's thoughts and viewpoint
- use well-chosen quotations from the poem to support your points on theme, content, language and structure
- explore comparisons and links that you can make between this war poem and other texts with similar themes.

Poem Glossary

Conscript: someone signed up for compulsory military service
Indifferent: uninterested
Flippant: disrespectfully light-hearted
Earnest: serious
Monocle: eyeglass for one eye
Cadaverous: gaunt and pale

The Conscript

by Wilfrid Gibson

Activity 1

First thoughts

'The Conscript' was written during the First World War. Conscription – where men are legally obliged to enrol for military service – was introduced in early 1916.

What are your first impressions of:

- the men waiting for their medical inspection?
- the doctors who inspect them?
- their attitudes to the soldiers and the war?

Activity 2

Looking more closely

1 In stanza 1, Gibson writes about the doctors' 'hasty award'.
 a What are the doctors awarding the men?
 b What does the word 'hasty' suggest?
 c Why do you think Gibson has chosen the word 'award'?

2 a Look at the description of the doctors in the first line. What does each word suggest about them?
 b Look at the description of the decision the doctors must make. It: 'Means life or death, maybe, or the living death'
 Compare this with the poem's first line. How has Gibson used these two lines to influence your response to the doctors?

3 Giving each man the results of his medical,
 'the chairman, as his monocle falls again,
 Pronounces each doom with easy indifferent breath.'
 a What does the word 'doom' suggest to you?
 b How does Gibson's description of the chairman's attitude influence your view of him?
 c The chairman is wearing a monocle. Why do you think Gibson has included this description?

4 Gibson describes the 'living death' of:
 'mangled limbs, blind eyes, or a darkened brain'
 What do you think Gibson means by a 'darkened brain'?

5 a The young man in stanza 2 is described standing 'wearily' and as being 'Cadaverous'. What does Gibson's choice of language suggest about this young man's life so far?
 b Gibson then adds 'as one already dead'. Does this add to your picture of the young man's past – or his future?

6 a How does the narrator react to the sight of this young man?
 b How do the doctors respond to him?
 c Do you find this surprising? Why?

Activity 3

Developing your ideas

1 a In stanza 1, Gibson describes the 'naked white / Bodies of men'. You might expect him to phrase this as 'men's naked white bodies'. What is the effect of Gibson's choice of word order?
  b Gibson focuses on one specific man in stanza 2. Why do you think he chooses to do this?

2 Mostly, the narrator describes what he sees. However, at the start of stanza 2, he describes his reaction: 'suddenly I shudder'. What effect do you think Gibson is trying to create here?

3 a Find five examples of negative language in the poem.
  b Find five examples of positive language.
  c What are Gibson's expectations for these men's futures?

Activity 4

Developing a personal response

1 a At the end of the poem, Gibson describes the young man 'With arms outstretched' and 'thorn-crowned' with 'nail-marks'. Why do you think Gibson is comparing the young man to Jesus Christ on the cross?
  - He is being unfairly punished.
  - He is sacrificing himself for others.
  - War is like the barbaric torture of crucifixion.
  - Something else?

  b How does this comparison affect your response to the doctors?

2 We are not told whether the doctors pass this young man fit for military service. Why do you think Gibson chooses not to reveal this?

Peer/Self-assessment

1 Answer true or false to the following statements.
  I can find evidence for and comment on:
  a Gibson's presentation of the doctors
  b Gibson's presentation of the men in stanza 1
  c Gibson's presentation of the man in stanza 2
  d Gibson's choice of language and its effects
  e Gibson's view of war, conscription and the men forced to fight
  f my response to the poem.

2 If you answered 'false' to any statements, compare your ideas with a partner's. Look again at the poem and your answers to the questions on these pages to help you.

3 What else can you say about this poem? Write a new set of true/false statements to assess a partner's understanding of 'The Conscript'.

4 a Write two paragraphs responding to the task:
  How are attitudes to war presented in 'The Conscript'?
  b Look at the grade descriptors on pages 148–155. What grade would you award your response?

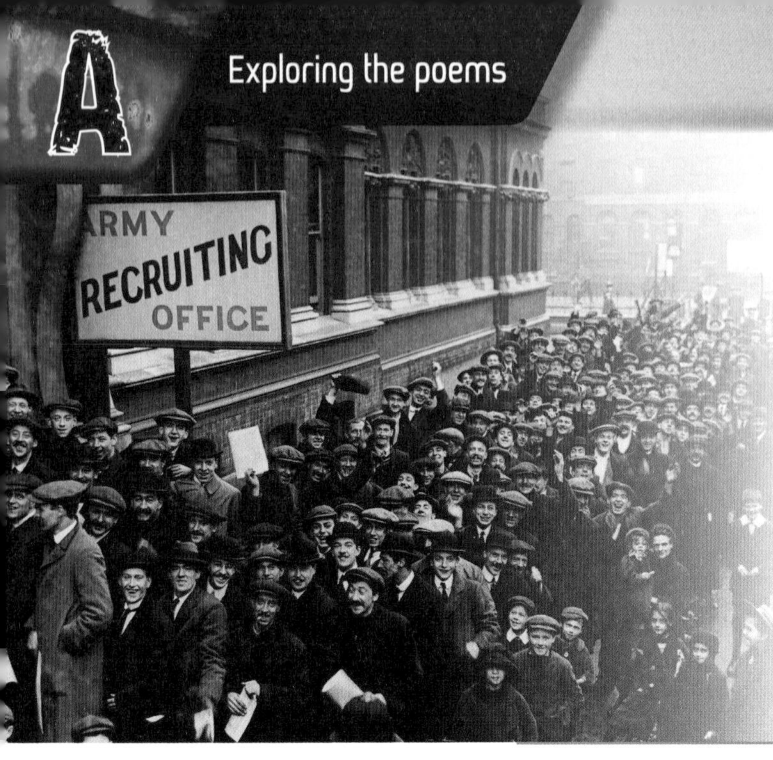

MCMXIV

by Philip Larkin

First thoughts

Activity 1

1 'MCMXIV' is about 1914, the year in which the First World War broke out, but was written in 1960. What do you think might have inspired Larkin to write the poem 46 years later?

2 Is 'MCMXIV' what you expect a war poem to be like? Write a sentence or two explaining your answer.

Looking more closely

Activity 2

1 Larkin writes about men queuing to enlist for the army, comparing them to men queuing to watch a game of cricket at The Oval, or football at Villa Park.
 a What does this suggest the men expect war to be like?
 b How does this contrast with the reality of the First World War?

2 Look again at stanza 1. What other evidence can you find that the men have no idea what war will be like?

3 Larkin writes about the 'countryside not caring', describing 'flowering grasses, and fields'. How does this contribute to Larkin's snapshot of Britain on the eve of war?

4 Larkin writes of the 'fields / Shadowing Domesday lines'. The Domesday Book was commissioned by William the Conqueror in 1086, 20 years after he invaded England. It was a kind of survey of his new kingdom, recording all its land, boundaries, landowners, workers and livestock.
 a Why do you think Larkin refers to this?
 b Domesday has another meaning. What is its significance here?

5 In the final stanza Larkin suggests that the period before the First World War was a time of innocence. He describes the men who went off to fight 'Leaving the gardens tidy'. What does this suggest about:
 a the men's attitude to the war
 b how long they thought they would be away?

6 Larkin goes on to write about: 'The thousands of marriages / Lasting a little while longer'
 a How will these thousands of marriages soon come to an end?
 b Why do you think Larkin has chosen to express this idea in this way?
 c Why has Larkin chosen to use the phrase 'a little while longer'?

My learning objectives

- to explore the themes of the poem, including conflict
- to develop my response to Larkin's poem
- to assess my work on Larkin's poem against the criteria in Assessment Objective 2 (page 134).

GradeStudio

MAKE THE GRADE

Examiner tips

You can achieve a high grade if you:

- make detailed reference to the language and structure Larkin uses to convey the narrator's thoughts and create the mood of the poem
- use well-chosen quotations from the poem to support your points on theme, content, language and structure
- explore comparisons and links that you can make between this war poem and other texts with similar themes.

Poem Glossary

MCMXIV: 1914
Archaic: out-dated
Farthings and sovereigns: old-fashioned coins
Twist: chewing tobacco

Activity 3

Developing your ideas

1 In stanza 4, Larkin writes about the 'innocence' of 1914 which, because of the war, 'changed itself to past' and was lost. Look at the following details from the poem.

'The Oval or Villa Park'

'farthings and sovereigns'

'hats'

'dark-clothed children at play
Called after kings and queens'

'moustached … faces'

'tin advertisements
For cocoa and twist'

'August Bank Holiday lark'

'the pubs
Wide open all day'

'shops, the bleached
Established names on the sunblinds'

'servants
With tiny rooms in huge houses'

a Which of these details makes you think that life in 1914 was just the same as it is now?
b Which of these details are just old-fashioned and describe the way life was in 1914?
c Which of these details from the poem make you think that 1914 was a time of innocence, very different from now?

2 a How many different sentences has Larkin used in this poem (try counting the full stops)?
b Look at the punctuation Larkin has used to divide the poem into images and stanzas. What effect does it create?

Activity 4

Developing a personal response

1 What – if anything – does the poem suggest to you about Larkin's attitude to:
a the queuing men
b the playing children
c those people whose marriages will last only 'a little while longer'
d the servants in their tiny rooms in huge houses
e the past
f war?

Make sure you use evidence from the poem to support your answers.

2 What is the dominant tone of the poem:
- nostalgia
- sadness
- sympathy
- regret
- horror
- impending doom
- happiness
- something else?

Write a sentence or two giving evidence and explaining your answer.

Peer/Self-assessment

1 Write two paragraphs responding to the task:
How does Larkin present the effects of war in 'MCMXIV'?
2 Look at the grade descriptors on pages 148–155. What grade would you award your response?
3 What could you change or add to improve your response? Use the grade descriptors to identify the two things most likely to improve your grade.
4 Redraft your answer, trying to make those changes.
5 Look again at the grade descriptors. Have you improved your grade?

The Charge of the Light Brigade

by Alfred, Lord Tennyson

My learning objectives

- to explore the themes of the poem, including conflict
- to develop my response to Tennyson's poem
- to assess my work on Tennyson's poem against the criteria in Assessment Objective 2 (page 134).

GradeStudio

Examiner tips

You can achieve a high grade if you:

- make detailed reference to the language and structure Tennyson uses to convey the narrator's thoughts and viewpoint
- use well-chosen quotations from the poem to support your points on theme, content, language and structure
- explore comparisons and links that you can make between this war poem and other texts with similar themes.

Poem Glossary

Light Brigade: a cavalry brigade in the British army
League: measurement of length, about 3 miles (5 km)
Battery: group of guns
Cossak: soldier on the Russian side
Sundered: separated

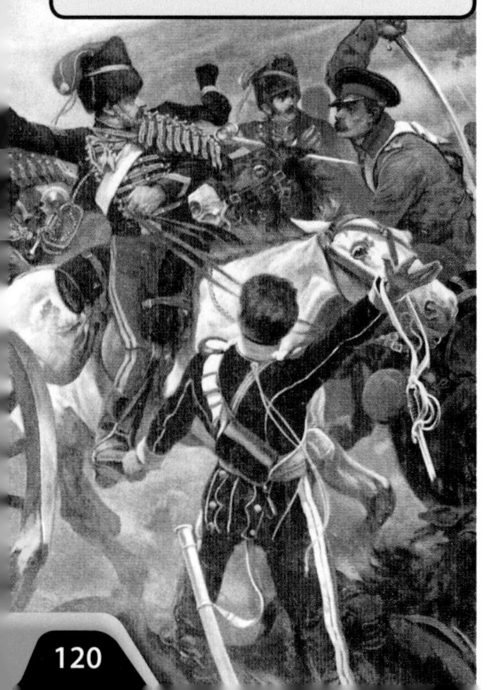

First thoughts

Activity 1

Tennyson wrote 'The Charge of the Light Brigade' in 1854, taking the details from a report in *The Times* newspaper. The poem is about the Battle of Balaclava, in the Crimean War (1853–56) in which England, France, Turkey, and Sardinia fought against Russia.

1. **a** Do you think the charge that Tennyson describes was a great success?
   b Who or what does he suggest was responsible for this?
2. What picture of war does the poem present?

Looking more closely

Activity 2

1. **a** What is happening at the very start of the poem?
   b What effect do you think Tennyson wants to create here?
2. Re-read stanza 2. Tennyson admits that the charge was a mistake when he writes 'Someone had blundered'.
   a Were the men of the Light Brigade aware of the mistake?
   b How did this affect their actions?
   c How does this affect your response to these soldiers?
3. In stanza 3, the focus of the narrative moves away from the soldiers' thoughts. What is the poem concentrating on here?
4. Look at stanza 4.
   'Cossack and Russian
   Reeled from the sabre-stroke
   Shattered and sundered.'
   Then look at this line from the end of stanza 4:
   'Then they rode back, but not,
   Not the six hundred.'
   a What has happened by the end of this stanza?
   b How does this contrast with the rest of the stanza?
   c Which elements of the battle is Tennyson concentrating on most closely in this stanza?
5. Re-read stanza 5 and compare it with stanza 3.
   a What similarities do you notice?
   b What differences do you notice?
   c How do these differences change the mood of the poem?
   d Why do you think Tennyson chose to make these two stanzas so similar?
6. In the final stanza, Tennyson directly addresses the reader. What response is he trying to create?

Developing your ideas

Activity 3

1 a Identify what Tennyson tells us about:
- the person who gave the order for this disastrous charge
- the enemy.

b What do you notice?

c What does this suggest about Tennyson's attitude to the charge of the Light Brigade?

2 a Identify all the verbs Tennyson uses to describe the battle. For example:
'Rode' 'Charge' 'thundered'

b How would you describe his choice of vocabulary?

c What effect is it intended to have on the reader?

3 Tennyson uses a range of linguistic and structural features to achieve his intended effect.

a Select evidence for each of the features below and match them with the appropriate comments about their effects.

Features	Effect created
• Repetition	To emphasise the heroism of the soldiers
• Metaphor	To emphasise the danger the soldiers are in
• Rhetorical questions	To create a sense of the inevitability of death
• Small number of rhymes used throughout	To suggest the pace of the battle
• Fast-paced, regular rhythm	To create a sense of excitement and adventure in the reader
	To draw the reader into the soldiers' experience and the poet's point of view
	To paint a powerful image of the danger and terror of battle
	To reflect the action being described

b Now write a sentence about each of the comments you selected, explaining *how* you think each feature creates this effect.

4 Do you think Tennyson approves of war?

Developing a personal response

Activity 4

Do you agree with Tennyson that we should 'Honour the Light Brigade'?

Peer/Self-assessment

1 Write two paragraphs responding to the task:
How does Tennyson present war in 'The Charge of the Light Brigade'?

2 Look at the grade descriptors on pages 148–155. What grade would you award your response?

3 What could you change or add to improve your response? Use the grade descriptors to identify the two things most likely to improve your grade.

4 Redraft your answer, trying to make those changes.

5 Look again at the grade descriptors. Have you improved your grade?

My learning objectives

- to explore the themes of the poem, including conflict
- to develop my response to Owen's poem
- to assess my work on Owen's poem against the criteria in Assessment Objective 2 (page 134).

GradeStudio

Examiner tips

You can achieve a high grade if you:

- make detailed reference to the language and structure Owen uses to convey the narrator's thoughts and viewpoint, and create the mood of the poem
- use well-chosen quotations from the poem to support your points on theme, content, language and structure
- explore comparisons and links that you can make between this war poem and other texts with similar themes.

Poem Glossary

Siding-shed: building in which trains are kept when not in use
Gay: cheerful
Spray: small bunch of flowers

The Send-Off

by Wilfred Owen

Activity 1

First thoughts

'The Send-Off' was written in 1918 while Owen was recovering from shell-shock at an army camp. It describes soldiers beginning their journey to the battle front.

1 **a** What is the usual mood of a send-off?
b What is the mood of this send-off? Why?

Activity 2

Looking more closely

1 Re-read stanza 1. Look at the vocabulary Owen chooses to describe the scene:
'close' 'darkening' 'lanes' 'sang' 'the siding-shed' 'grimly gay'
Write a sentence or two commenting on:
- the effect of each of Owen's choices
- their combined effect.

2 In stanza 2, Owen describes the flowers that well-wishers have given to the soldiers.
a What is the difference between a 'wreath' and a 'spray' of flowers?
b The word 'stuck' can mean *fixed*, but also *pierced*. What does each of these meanings suggest about the flowers?

3 Think of any films or television programmes you have seen showing soldiers going off to war. Who is watching in 'The Send-Off' as the soldiers leave? What effect is created?

4 Re-read stanza 4.
a Owen personifies the railway signals. He says they 'nodded' although they are 'unmoved'. What does this suggest about the signals' attitude to the soldiers and their fate?
b Owen also personifies the lamp with which the driver signals to the guard, saying that it 'winked'. What does this suggest?

5 In stanza 5 Owen makes his views clearer. What does each line of this stanza tell you about Owen's view of the war?

6 **a** What is Owen suggesting in the poem's last three lines?
b Look at the way he expresses this idea:
'A few, a few, too few' 'drums and yells' 'creep back' 'silent' 'village wells' 'half-known roads'
Choose three of these words or phrases and write a sentence or two for each, commenting on the effect created.

Developing your ideas

Activity 3

1 In stanza 2, Owen writes:
'Their breasts were stuck all white with wreath and spray
As men's are, dead.'
He might have written:
as men's breasts are when they are dead'
Why do you think he chose to shorten this line and place the final word after a comma?

2 Look at some of the other short lines in the poem.
   a What do you notice about the language used in these lines?
   b What effect is Owen trying to create?

3 a How would you describe the prevailing mood of the poem?
   b Can you identify any language that contrasts with this mood?
   c How does Owen use this contrasting language?

Developing a personal response

Activity 4

1 How do you respond to Owen's description of these men? Use two or three quotations to support your answer.

2 Identify three words or phrases from the poem that are important in creating your response.

Peer/Self-assessment

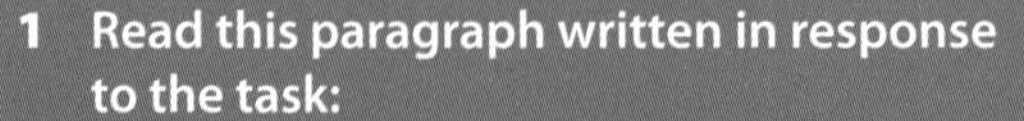

1 **Read this paragraph written in response to the task:**
How does Owen express his point of view in 'The Send-Off'?

2 **Write a paragraph giving your own response to the task. Use the same structure as the paragraph on the right.**

3 **Annotate your paragraph using the same notes as the paragraph on the right. If you have forgotten to include anything in your paragraph, add it in.**

4 **Which criteria in Assessment Objective 2 on page 134 have you demonstrated in your paragraph?**

Evidence to support the point

A clear point

Owen describes the soldiers' departure for the front by train:
'Then, unmoved, signals nodded, and a lamp
Winked to the guard.'
Owen is personifying the signals, suggesting that they are actively sending the men off to war. The word 'nodded' implies that they approve of this action, and despite physically moving they are 'unmoved' and do not care. The word 'winked' implies some kind of conspiracy: as if everyone apart from the soldiers knows what awaits them. Owen is portraying the men as innocent victims, like lambs going to slaughter, making them seem even more vulnerable.

An explanation of the effect of the quotation

How language reflects the poet's point of view

Close focus on particular word choice

The Man He Killed

by Thomas Hardy

My learning objectives

- to explore the themes of the poem, including conflict
- to develop my response to Hardy's poem
- to assess my work on Hardy's poem against the criteria in Assessment Objective 2 (page 134).

GradeStudio

Examiner tips

You can achieve a high grade if you:

- make detailed reference to the language and structure Hardy uses to convey the narrator's thoughts
- use well-chosen quotations from the poem to support your points on theme, content, language and structure
- explore comparisons and links that you can make between this war poem and other texts with similar themes.

Poem Glossary

Wet: drink
Nipperkin: small glass of beer
'list: enlist, join the army
Traps: belongings, particularly tools
Quaint: peculiar, funny
Half a crown: coin (of quite high value to a poor person)

First thoughts

Activity 1

1 The poem is spoken by the voice of a narrator. Who do you think is the narrator?

2 What is the narrator's attitude to war?

Looking more closely

Activity 2

1 Re-read the first two stanzas of the poem.
   a Who is the 'he' that the narrator imagines enjoying a drink with?
   b How did the two men actually meet?

2 In stanza 3, the narrator explains why he did what he did. Look at the phrases he uses: 'Just so', 'of course', 'That's clear enough'. All of these have a similar meaning. What do they suggest the narrator is thinking?

3 Re-read stanza 4. Are the following statements true or false? Use evidence from the poem to support your answers.
   The narrator imagines that the other man joined the army because …
   a he wanted to fight for his country
   b he did it without really thinking
   c he needed the money
   d he strongly believed that it was a cause worth fighting for.

4 One of the reasons the narrator imagines caused the other man to join the army is because he had 'sold his traps'.
   a What does this mean he can no longer do?
   b Why do you think he 'sold his traps'?

5 a How does the narrator guess the details about the man he killed?
   b How does this add to the power of the poem?

Developing your ideas

Activity 3

1 The narrator of the poem talks directly to the reader. How has Hardy achieved this effect, using language and punctuation?

2 a What do we learn about the narrator of the poem? Think about:
- what he says
- the ways he says it
- what he tells us about himself.

b Why do you think Hardy chose this kind of character as the narrator?

3 a Look carefully at the structure of stanza 3, as the narrator tries to explain why he killed a man. What effect does each of the writer's choices have? Match the writer's choices to the effect created.

Writer's choice	Effect created
• At the end of the first line there is a dash • The word 'because' is repeated • There is repetitive internal rhyme • The word 'although' is left dangling at the end of the stanza	• It suggests the narrator may be about to question his own explanation • It increases the pace of the line, suggesting the narrator is hurrying because even he is not convinced by his explanation • It suggests hesitation. Can the narrator really explain what he did? • It signals a pause, suggesting the narrator does not know what to say

b What is the combined effect of all these features?

4 The poem is written in the first person, so you might expect the poem to be called 'The Man I Killed'. Why do you think Hardy chose to call it 'The Man **He** Killed?'

Developing a personal response

Activity 4

1 Do you agree with the narrator that war is 'quaint and curious'?

2 Do you think Thomas Hardy agrees with the narrator?

Peer/Self-assessment

Read this paragraph, written in response to a task exploring the theme of conflict:
How does Hardy present war in 'The Man He Killed'?

1 Write a paragraph giving your own response to the task. Use the same structure as the paragraph on the right.

2 Annotate your paragraph using the same notes as the paragraph on the right. If you have forgotten to include anything in your paragraph, add it in.

3 Which criteria in Assessment Objective 2 (page 134) have you demonstrated in your paragraph?

Evidence to support the point

A clear point

The narrator speaks directly to the reader:
'You shoot a fellow down
You'd treat if met where any bar is.'
Hardy has placed the entire poem in quotation marks to emphasise that the narrator is talking directly to us, as if it is us having a nipperkin with him in an ancient inn. The language the narrator uses, such as 'fellow' and 'treat', is simple and informal. Hardy is using the voice of the narrator to make his point that ordinary men do not want to fight and kill; they only do it because they are told to.

An explanation of the effect of the quotation

How it reflects the poet's point of view

Close focus on the writer's choice

My learning objectives

- to explore the themes of the poem, including conflict
- to develop my response to Hardy's poem
- to assess my work on Hardy's poem against the criteria in Assessment Objective 2 (page 134).

GradeStudio

Examiner tips

You can achieve a high grade if you:
- make detailed reference to the language and structure Hardy uses to convey the narrator's thoughts and viewpoint
- use well-chosen quotations from the poem to support your points on theme, content, language and structure
- explore comparisons and links that you can make between this war poem and other texts with similar themes.

Poem Glossary

Kopje-crest: (Afrikaans) small hill
Veldt: (Afrikaans) plain; flat, open ground
Wessex: old term for southwest England
Karoo: (Afrikaans) region in South Africa
Bush: large area of wilderness
Loam: soil

Drummer Hodge

by Thomas Hardy

First thoughts

Activity 1

Until the twentieth century, the British army recruited boys as young as ten to be drummer boys. They not only provided a marching and morale-boosting beat; their different drum rolls were used to give commands on the battlefield. 'Drummer Hodge' was first published in 1899, just weeks into the Second Boer War (1899–1902) in which the Boers fought the British for control of South Africa.

1 How do you think Hardy wants the reader to respond to the death in conflict of Drummer Hodge?

2 Why do you think Hardy chose to write about the death of a drummer boy to achieve this response?

Looking more closely

Activity 2

1 In the first line, Hardy tells us 'They throw in Drummer Hodge'. Who do you think 'they' might be? Why aren't we told?

2 What would you expect a fallen soldier's burial to be like? How does this differ?

3 **a** What do we learn about the character of Hodge?
  b What do the words 'homely' and 'Fresh' suggest?

4 What does Hardy imagine happening to Hodge's corpse, now buried in South Africa?

5 Hardy describes Hodge as 'Northern' because Wessex is in the northern hemisphere, and South Africa as 'Southern' because it is in the southern hemisphere. What effect is Hardy trying to create?

6 Hardy uses terms from the Afrikaans language (the language of the Boers, the rulers of South Africa) to describe where Hodge is buried. What effect does this have?

7 Hardy refers to the stars three times in the poem. What is their significance in:
  a stanza 1?
  b stanza 2?
  c stanza 3?

Developing your ideas

Activity 3

1 **a** What do we learn from the poem about the battle in which Hodge died, and his death?
  b Why do you think Hardy made this decision?

2 Each stanza of the poem is written in a different tense.
   a Match the stanza to the tense:

Stanza	Tense
1	Future
2	Present
3	Past

   b What is surprising about the order in which Hardy tells Hodge's story?
   c Why do you think Hardy chose to do this?

3 The language of the poem is quite simple. Its structure is also simple and follows a straightforward pattern.
   a How does this reflect what the poem is about?
   b How does it affect your response to the poem?

Developing a personal response

Activity 4

1 In stanza 2, Hardy tells us how little Hodge knew of the land where he died – but by the end of the poem he has become a part of it. Does this make the brutality of his burial any better?

2 Hardy contrasts human actions following Hodge's death with nature's response to it. Why do you think he has chosen to do this?

Peer/Self-assessment

MAKE THE GRADE

1 **Answer true or false to the following statements.**
   I can find evidence for and comment on:
   a the character of Drummer Hodge
   b the way in which Hodge is buried
   c the details Hardy chooses to include in the poem – and those he chooses to leave out
   d the role of nature in the poem
   e Hardy's choice of language and its effects
   f Hardy's choice of structure and its effects
   g my response to the poem.

2 If you answered 'false' to any statements, compare your ideas with a partner's. Look again at the poem and your answers to the questions on these pages to help you.

3 What else can you say about this poem? Write a new set of true/false statements to assess a partner's understanding of 'Drummer Hodge'.

4 a Write two paragraphs responding to the task:
   How does Hardy present his attitude to the casualties of war in 'Drummer Hodge'?
   b Look at the grade descriptors on pages 148–155. What grade would you award your response?

The Hero

by Siegfried Sassoon

First thoughts

Activity 1

This poem is about a death in the First World War.

1 How did Jack die, according to what the Brother Officer has told the Mother, and the letter she has received?

2 How does the Brother Officer think Jack really died?

3 Which version do you think Sassoon wants us to believe?

Looking more closely

Activity 2

1 Look at the Mother's reaction to news of her son's death in stanza 1. How does she feel?

2 The Brother Officer says he has told the Mother some lies that she will 'nourish'. What does this word suggest to you?

3 **a** Why do you think Sassoon refers to him as the Brother Officer?
b Is this an appropriate title for him?

4 In the final stanza, Sassoon describes how Jack died. What impression does this give you of life in the trenches?

5 The Brother Officer describes Jack as 'cold-footed'. What do you think he means?

6 The Brother Officer tells us about Jack's efforts to escape the war:

'how he'd tried
To get sent home, and how, at last, he died'

Does the phrase 'at last' imply:

- it was bound to happen sooner or later because he was trying to get wounded and sent home
- death is inevitable for these soldiers
- Jack was trying to get killed
- something else?

How does your chosen interpretation affect your response to the character of Jack?

7 The Mother in the poem is described by the Brother Officer in stanza 2 as 'the poor old dear' and at the end of the poem as 'that lonely woman with white hair'.
a What does each of these descriptions suggest about the attitude of the Brother Officer?
b How does his attitude change?
c How does this affect your response to the poem?

8 Why do you think Sassoon chose the title 'The Hero'?

My learning objectives

- to explore the themes of the poem, including conflict
- to develop my response to Sassoon's poem
- to assess my work on Sassoon's poem against the criteria in Assessment Objective 2 (page 134).

GradeStudio

MAKE THE GRADE

Examiner tips

You can achieve a high grade if you:

- make detailed reference to the language and structure Sassoon uses to convey the narrator's thoughts and viewpoint
- use well-chosen quotations from the poem to support your points on theme, content, language and structure
- explore comparisons and links that you can make between this war poem and other texts with similar themes.

Developing your ideas

Activity 3

1 There are four characters in the poem, yet only one is named. The others are referred to according to their relationship with Jack. Why do you think Sassoon has chosen to do this?

2 When the Brother Officer refers to Jack, his name is in inverted commas. What does this suggest about the officer's attitude to Jack?

3 Look at how Sassoon describes Jack's death: 'Blown to small bits'.
   a What is the effect of Sassoon's description?
   b Which of these do you feel contributes most to the effect:
   - it uses simple, monosyllabic language
   - it is a very blunt ending to a long sentence
   - it is positioned at the start of a line
   - its language is almost childish
   - something else?

Developing a personal response

Activity 4

1 Think about the three main characters in the poem.
   a How do you respond to Jack?
   b How do you respond to the Mother?
   c How do you respond to the Brother Officer?
   Choose evidence from the poem to support your responses.

2 Look at this range of different responses to the task:
   How does Sassoon present his view of war in 'The Hero'?
   - Sassoon feels sorry for the relatives of soldiers killed in action.
   - Sassoon thinks that many soldiers described as heroes are actually cowards.
   - Sassoon thinks that fear is a normal human reaction to the horrors of war.
   - Sassoon dislikes officers who do not respect other soldiers.
   - Sassoon hates the hypocrisy and lies of war.
   - Sassoon feels that war and death are not glorious.

   Turn three of these responses into point-evidence-explanation paragraphs by:
   - finding evidence for each response
   - adding a sentence or two explaining how and why your evidence supports each response.

Peer/Self-assessment

1 **Look at your answer to question 2 in Activity 4 above, and at the grade descriptors on pages 148–155. What grade would you award your answer?**
2 **What could you change or add to improve your response? Use the grade descriptors to identify the two things most likely to improve your grade.**
3 **Redraft your answer, trying to make those changes.**
4 **Look again at the grade descriptors. Have you improved your grade?**

Section B: Tackling the task

Approaching the controlled assessment

The controlled assessment is a single assignment linking a Shakespeare play with Literary Heritage poetry.

The WJEC GCSE English Literature specification states that you must 'show appreciation of poetry chosen from a range studied during the course from the WJEC Poetry Collection, and of a play by Shakespeare'. Note that in English Literature, you will not be permitted to answer on the Shakespeare plays that are on the external examination list.

The texts chosen must be linked by a theme (listed below). Your assignment must consider the ways in which the theme is explored in **both** the poetry and the Shakespeare play.

The Board will list the poems to be studied in any particular year in the specifications.

Themes

Here is the list of themes that you *may* be asked to write about, with suggestions for suitable poetry choices listed underneath:

LOVE
'The Passionate Shepherd to His Love' by Christopher Marlowe
'The Sun Rising' by John Donne
'Cousin Kate' by Christina Rossetti
'Sonnet 18' by William Shakespeare
'Sonnet 43' by Elizabeth Barrett Browning
'Valentine' by Carol Ann Duffy
'A Frosty Night' by Robert Graves
'The Flea' by John Donne
'Holy Sonnet 17' by John Donne

FAMILY AND PARENT/CHILD RELATIONSHIPS
'Long Distance II' by Tony Harrison
'Catrin' by Gillian Clarke
'Follower' by Seamus Heaney
'What has Happened to Lulu?' by Charles Causley
'Mid-Term Break' by Seamus Heaney
'The Almond Tree' by Jon Stallworthy
'Prayer Before Birth' by Louis MacNeice
'On My First Son' by Ben Jonson
'My Grandmother' by Elizabeth Jennings

YOUTH AND AGE
'My Heart is Like a Withered Nut!' by Caroline Norton
'Old Age Gets Up' by Ted Hughes
'Sweet 18' by Sheenagh Pugh
'Do Not Go Gentle Into That Good Night' by Dylan Thomas
'Crabbed Age and Youth' by William Shakespeare

POWER AND AMBITION
'Porphyria's Lover' by Robert Browning
'I Have Longed to Move Away' by Dylan Thomas
'Leisure' by W. H. Davies
'Human Interest' by Carol Ann Duffy
'Hawk Roosting' by Ted Hughes
'My Last Duchess' by Robert Browning
'Ozymandias' by Percy Bysshe Shelley
'The Interrogation' by Edwin Muir

MALE/FEMALE RELATIONSHIPS AND THE ROLE OF WOMEN
'They Did Not Expect This' by Vernon Scannell
'Meeting Point' by Louis MacNeice
'Afternoons' by Philip Larkin
'Havisham' by Carol Ann Duffy
'To the Virgins, To Make Much of Time' by Robert Herrick
'To His Coy Mistress' by Andrew Marvell
'Song: The Willing Mistriss' by Aphra Behn
'A Woman to Her Lover' by Christina Walsh
'Twice Shy' by Seamus Heaney
'The Beggar Woman' by William King
'Whoso List to Hunt' by Sir Thomas Wyatt
'Sonnet 116' by William Shakespeare
'Sonnet 130' by William Shakespeare
'Song of the Worker's Wife' by Alice Gray Jones
'A Married State' by Katherine Philips

HYPOCRISY AND PREJUDICE
'Chapel Deacon' by R. S. Thomas
'The Hunchback in the Park' by Dylan Thomas
'Displaced Person Looks at a Cage-bird' by D. J. Enright
'Base Details' by Siegfried Sassoon
'The Capon Clerk' by Sheenagh Pugh
'You Will Be Hearing From Us Shortly' by U. A. Fanthorpe
'Refugee Blues' by W. H. Auden
'In Church' by Thomas Hardy

CONFLICT
'Dulce et Decorum Est' by Wilfred Owen
'A Refusal to Mourn the Death, by Fire, of a Child in London' by Dylan Thomas
'The Soldier' by Rupert Brooke
'The Conscript' by Wilfrid Gibson
'MCMXIV' by Philip Larkin
'The Charge of the Light Brigade' by Alfred Lord Tennyson
'The Send-Off' by Wilfred Owen
'The Man He Killed' by Thomas Hardy
'Drummer Hodge' by Thomas Hardy
'The Hero' by Siegfried Sassoon

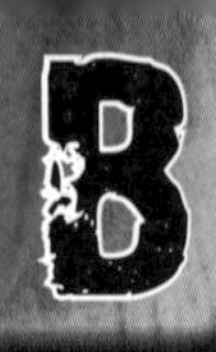

GRIEF
'Long Distance II' by Tony Harrison 'Mid-Term Break' by Seamus Heaney 'The Almond Tree' by Jon Stallworthy 'On My First Son' by Ben Jonson 'My Grandmother' by Elizabeth Jennings 'My Heart is Like a Withered Nut!' by Caroline Norton 'Havisham' by Carol Ann Duffy 'A Refusal to Mourn the Death, by Fire, of a Child in London' by Dylan Thomas 'The Hero' by Siegfried Sassoon

These suggestions are provided as a guide only. You will find that many of the poems address a number of themes. For example, look at 'Porphyria's Lover' by Robert Browning. This appears in the 'Power and Ambition' category above, but could also be in 'Male/female relationships and the role of women'. Could it also fit any other theme?

Activity

Look at the poems that you have studied. Which of them fit more than one category? Write your findings in a table like the one below:

Poem	Love	Family relationships	Youth/ Age	Power and ambition	Male/female relationships	Hypocrisy/ prejudice	Conflict	Grief
'Porphyria's Lover'				✓	✓			

As you work through the tasks on the poems in this book (in Section A), you will see questions prompting you to consider the theme. The final writing task on each poem also focuses on a theme in order to help you think about ways to link the poetry with your chosen Shakespeare text.

GradeStudio

MAKE THE GRADE

Examiner tips

You need to link your chosen Shakespeare text with a selection of poetry. They need to be linked by theme. As you are studying your Shakespeare text, make a note of the main themes arising. Which of the poems have the same theme(s)?

Introduction to the tasks

Look at this typical controlled assessment task:

> Many plays and poems are concerned with the relationship between youth and age. Choose one relationship between a young and old person in the Shakespeare play you have studied and link it with the way a similar relationship is presented in your chosen poems.

You will see that this question does not specify any particular play or poems. You need to apply this question to the play you have been studying in class, and choose poetry from the Poetry Collection that fits this theme.

Your work will need to be structured in three distinct sections:

Write about the Shakespeare play in relation to the theme

Write about your chosen poems in relation to the theme

Discuss your personal feelings about the texts, and make links and comparisons between them

Here is an example of how the question can be adapted to suit the play you are studying:

> **Theme: Youth and age**
>
> - Write about the way Shakespeare presents the relationship between youth and age in *Romeo and Juliet*. You may wish to focus on the relationship between Capulet and his daughter, Juliet.
> - William Shakespeare's poem 'Crabbed Age and Youth' is also concerned with the relationship between youth and age. Write about the way Shakespeare presents this theme. In your answer you should also refer to other poetry that links to this theme.
> - What is your response to the pieces of literature? Try to make links between them.

Before we look at a typical task and how each of the bullet points should be tackled, you should familiarise yourself with the Assessment Objectives that are used to grade your work. These objectives are detailed on page 134. Also, you will find grade checklists in the Grade Studio on pages 148–155, which will help you to identify the grade you are currently working at and show you how you may progress up the grade ladder.

Assessment Objectives

Note on GCSE English

For English only, you will be required to show that you are aware of the 'social, cultural and historical' contexts of the play and poem(s). This means that you will need to:

- show an understanding of the period in which the text is set
- show an understanding of the period in which the text was written
- show an understanding of how the life and times of the writer may have influenced his or her work.

This means looking not just at the play/poem and what happens in it, but being aware of things that may have influenced the writer. For example, it means looking at a character as an individual, but also being aware of aspects such as his or her nationality, religion or generation.

Consider the following areas when reading your poem(s) and play:

- When is the text set? Is that different from when it was written?
- What does society appear to be like?
- Is there anything to say about the setting or location of the text? How might these factors have influenced the text?

GradeStudio

Examiner tip

Although you need to have an awareness of these issues, **the texts themselves must be the main focus of your discussion**. You should mention events in the life of the author, or aspects of the historical period, **only** where these are relevant to what you have to say about the text.

Assessment Objectives: English Literature	Weighting
AO1 • Respond to the texts giving careful and thoughtful opinions • Select short quotations from the texts to support your ideas • Discuss quotations and analyse their meaning	6.25%
AO2 • Discuss how the writers use language, structure and form to present ideas • Discuss the theme of the texts	6.25%
AO3 • Make links between the texts • Write about the similarities and differences of the texts • Write about the writers' different ways of expressing meaning and achieving effects	12.5%
Percentage of final mark	**25%**

Assessment Objectives: English	Weighting
AO2 • Respond to the texts giving careful and thoughtful opinions • Select short quotations from the texts to support your ideas • Discuss quotations and analyse their meaning • Discuss how the writers use language, structure and form to present ideas and themes • Make links between the texts • Write about the similarities and differences of the texts • Demonstrate an understanding of the period in which the texts are set • Demonstrate an understanding of how the life and times of the writer may have influenced his or her work	10%
Percentage of final mark	**10%**

What the tasks require

Whichever texts you study, you will find that the structure of the controlled assessment question will be the same.

For example, here is another typical question:

The **theme** is the key to linking the Shakespeare text and poem. The play and poem will have similarities and differences relating to this theme.

Theme: Love

- Write about the way Shakespeare presents the theme of love in *Romeo and Juliet*. Focus on the relationship between Romeo and Juliet.
- Christopher Marlowe's poem 'The Passionate Shepherd to His Love' is also concerned with the theme of love. Write about the way love is presented in this poem. In your answer you should also refer to other poetry that links to this theme.
- What is your response to the pieces of literature? Try to make links between them.

The **first bullet point** will always ask you to write about the Shakespeare text in relation to the theme. The second part of this bullet point may ask you to consider a particular area of the text or, for example, a particular relationship.

The **second bullet point** will ask you to write about your chosen poetry in relation to the theme.

The **third bullet point** will ask you to give your own views on the texts. This is where you will need to draw links and comparisons between them, based on the theme. Look for similarities and differences between the texts.

Look at the questions on the following page. You will see that they all follow the same basic structure, even though the theme and texts are different:

Theme: Family and parent/child relationships

- Write about the way Shakespeare presents the theme of family in *Romeo and Juliet*. Write about the relationship between Juliet and her parents.
- Gillian Clarke's poem 'Catrin' is also concerned with the theme of parent/child relationships. Write about the way this theme is presented in the poem. In your answer you should also refer to other poetry that links to this theme.
- What is your response to the two pieces of literature? Try to make links between them.

This question suggests that you may initially want to focus on one particular area to give you a sharper focus

Theme: Male/female relationships and the role of women

- Look at the way Shakespeare presents Katherine's relationship with Petruchio in *The Taming of the Shrew*. Consider what Petruchio says about how women should behave and Katherine's reaction to his views.
- Christina Walsh also writes about the role of women in her poem 'A Woman to Her Lover'. Consider the ways she presents her views. In your answer you should also refer to other poetry that links to this theme.
- What is your personal response to the pieces of literature? Try to make links between them.

This question directs you to look at a specific aspect of the text

Theme: Grief

- Write about the way Shakespeare explores the theme of grief in *Hamlet*.
- Ben Jonson's poem 'On My First Son' also explores the feeling of grief after the death of his young son. Consider the way he presents his views. In your answer you should also refer to other poetry that links to this theme.
- What is your personal response to the pieces of literature? Try to make links between them.

This question has a broad scope and allows you to discuss any areas of the text that you consider relevant

Tackling Shakespeare in the controlled assessment

Your teacher will choose which Shakespeare play you study. It is important to remember that Shakespeare's plays, just like any other play, were not written to be read; they were written to be *performed*. If you can see the play being acted out, this will help you to understand it much better. If you cannot see the play live on stage, it is a good idea to watch a recording of it.

Shakespeare's theatre

It is also worth bearing in mind that the theatres in Shakespeare's day were very different from the ones we have today.

- There was no lighting other than candles, so plays had to be performed in daylight. There was also little scenery, so writers had to make the setting and the time of day clear through their language, to involve the audience in the scene.
- Women were not allowed to perform on stage, so female characters were played by boys.
- Theatres were very noisy places. Many audience members stood for the entire performance, eating snacks and drinking beer while watching. It was also common to move around to get a better view, or buy fruit and nuts from sellers wandering around the yard. The cheapest part of the theatre was the yard immediately surrounding the stage. This area was not covered, so if it rained the audience standing in the yard (the groundlings) got wet!
- Few props and a restricted range of costumes were used, so the actors had to convey character and action through dialogue and other speeches.

Shakespeare's language: Verse

Shakespeare's language differs from that of today, as the English language has changed enormously over the past 400 years. Shakespeare's plays are mainly written in verse (poetry), which was a popular form for plays at the time. The kind of verse that Shakespeare uses is called **blank verse**. Blank verse does not rhyme, but has a regular **metre**. Metre is the pattern of stressed and unstressed syllables that gives rhythm to a line of poetry. It is one way that a writer can structure language to make it more meaningful and memorable. Blank verse is very close in rhythm to natural speech, which makes it ideal for presenting dialogue.

The metre used in blank verse is called **iambic pentameter**. An **iamb** is an unstressed syllable followed by a stressed syllable. The word **pentameter** means that each line has five of these. So the basic pattern of blank verse is that each line has 10 syllables (five alternating unstressed and stressed beats).
Of course, the rhythm often varies from this basic, underlying pattern in order to achieve particular effects.

Look at the following lines from *Macbeth* and think about the rhythm. The symbol ˘ above a syllable means that it is unstressed, and the symbol / indicates that it is stressed.

So foul and fair a day I have not seen.

And all our yes ter days have light ed fools

The way to dus ty death. Out, out, brief can dle!

You will see in the final line quoted above that the rhythm changes with the words 'Out, out, brief candle!' – the repeated 'out' is given extra stress.

Shakespeare's language: Prose

As well as using blank verse, Shakespeare uses **prose** in his plays. Prose is often used for:

- comedy scenes (such as the scene with the Porter in *Macbeth*, Act 2 Scene 3)
- dialogue between characters of a low status (e.g. servants or drunkards), or of a very informal, vulgar or disrespectful type
- circumstances where a character is losing control or descending into madness (e.g. Lady Macbeth in Act 5 Scene 1)
- characters reading out letters or messages (e.g. Lady Macbeth in Act 1 Scene 5).

But there are no strict rules. Potentially all characters can switch between verse and prose depending on who they are talking to and what they are talking about.

GradeStudio

MAKE THE GRADE

Examiner tips

In order to decide why Shakespeare has chosen to use prose or verse, you should look at who is speaking, who the person is speaking to, what he or she is saying and why.

Activity

Look at the play you are studying and work out which characters speak in verse or prose, when and where this happens, and why Shakespeare may have chosen to do this.

Tackling your Shakespeare text

You must know and understand the **plot** (story) of the play you are studying. As you are reading the play, give each scene a title and make notes on each one to help you see how the play is *structured*.

You will notice that the play is written in five Acts. Each Act contains several Scenes.

The plots of Shakespeare's plays all follow this basic structure:

- **The main characters and the general situation are introduced.** The characters are reasonably in harmony with the world and each other.
- **Problems appear.** The harmony is disrupted and trouble arises.
- **The problems develop.** The world of the characters becomes more complex and threatens to descend into chaos.
- **Climax.** The dramatic tension reaches its highest point and the problems escalate to a crisis.
- **Ending.** Order and unity are restored.

Macbeth, for example, follows this structure:

- Macbeth and Banquo encounter three witches who prophesy that Macbeth will become king. Macbeth writes to his wife to inform her of this.
- Lady Macbeth, inspired by the letter, plots to help Macbeth become king. She persuades Macbeth that King Duncan must be killed when he stays with them for an overnight visit.
- Macbeth proceeds with the murder and becomes king, but is shaken by his crime. He resorts to further killings to cover up what he has done and to try to prevent the witches' other prophecy, that Banquo's descendants will be kings, from coming true. Lady Macbeth begins to break down under the strain of events.
- Macbeth becomes increasingly desperate and returns to the witches to question them about his fate. He is deserted by most of his followers, and an army led by the old king's son, Malcolm, is gathering against him. Lady Macbeth dies.
- Malcolm's English army is reinforced by Scots desperate to see an end to Macbeth's violent reign. Macbeth is killed and Malcolm is named king.

Activity

Look at the play you are studying and work out how it is structured, using the five-point outline on page 138.

Annotating the text

Your teacher will probably decide which scenes you will focus on for the controlled assessment. As you read your play, it is very helpful if you can annotate the text with ideas that will help you to explore the theme of your task.

For example, look at the following extract from *Macbeth*. It has been annotated with the theme of power and ambition in mind:

Act 1 Scene 5 lines 38–54

LADY MACBETH … The raven himself is hoarse
That croaks the fatal entrance of Duncan
Under my battlements. Come, you spirits
That tend on mortal thoughts, unsex me here,
And fill me from the crown to the toe top-full
Of direst cruelty; make thick my blood,
Stop up th'access and passage to remorse,
That no compunctious visitings of nature
Shake my fell purpose, nor keep peace between
Th'effect and it. Come to my woman's breasts,
And take my milk for gall, you murdering ministers,
Wherever in your sightless substances
You wait on nature's mischief. Come, thick night,
And pall thee in the dunnest smoke of hell,
That my keen knife see not the wound it makes,
Nor heaven peep through the blanket of the dark,
To cry, 'Hold, hold!'

Annotations:

- Bird of ill-omen. She is suggesting Duncan will meet his death very soon
- She is determined that Duncan's fate will be to be murdered
- She invokes demonic spirits to harden her determination and destroy any weakness or pity she may feel
- She wants her femininity to be taken away
- She is intent on committing evil
- She is prepared to swap life-giving milk for deathly poison
- She asks the powers of darkness to hide her intentions
- She intends to commit the murder herself

Tackling the controlled assessment task

Now that you understand how the tasks work and have studied your play and poems, it is time to think about the controlled assessment task itself. The following pages contain some exemplar student answers with examiner comments and tips. Studying these will help you to understand the mark scheme and move up the grade ladder.

It is useful to study the grade checklists on pages 148–155 because your work will be marked according to these. These checklists will help you to identify the grade you are currently working at, and show you what you need to do to reach the next grade.

Your grade relates to your work as a whole, but the following indicators and examples should give you an idea of the features of each grade. We shall be focusing on *Macbeth* and 'Hawk Roosting' by Ted Hughes in these sample responses, but the features of each grade remain the same for any text.

Tackling the first bullet point

The following section focuses on how to tackle the first bullet point of the question. The first bullet will always ask you to consider the Shakespeare text you are studying. This is where you will need to discuss your Shakespeare play in relation to the theme of the question.

Consider this question:

Theme: Power and ambition

- Write about the way Shakespeare presents the theme of power and ambition. Focus initially on the events leading up to the death of King Duncan, and the relationship between Macbeth and Lady Macbeth shortly after the murder.
- Ted Hughes's poem 'Hawk Roosting' is also concerned with the theme of power and ambition. Write about the way the hawk is presented. In your answer you should also refer to other poetry that links to this theme.
- What is your personal response to the pieces of literature? Try to make links between them.

This is the part of the question that we will focus on here – tackling the Shakespeare text

Look at the following extracts from answers to the first bullet point of the question above. One is a grade C response, and the other is a grade A response. Use the grade checklists on pages 148–155 to help you see the differences between the two grades.

C grade answer

Student A

Focus is immediately on the theme

Ambition is the main theme in Shakespeare's play *Macbeth*. We first learn that Macbeth is a loyal soldier, defending king and country in battle. After an encounter with three witches on his way home from battle, Macbeth's ambition becomes his weakness. He is influenced by the witches' prophecies, and then his wife's ambition for him, and starts out on a path to become the king …

Clear introduction, with some overview

Macbeth is affected by the witches. A big part of him believes in their power to see into the future and, although he knows they are evil, he begins to believe their words. This is where Macbeth allows his ambitious thoughts to take over. When he writes to his wife to tell her that the witches have predicted that he will become king one day, we can see that she is very ambitious too:

Clear focus on the question. The theme is clearly being addressed

Selecting and highlighting a key area

'Glamis thou art, and Cawdor, and shalt be
What thou art promised;'

Selecting individual words shows close focus on language

The word 'shalt' suggests that she is very confident that this can come true. We then learn that she thinks that Macbeth will not be able to achieve the power by himself because he is 'too full o' the milk of human kindness'. She thinks he will need her help to become king and so she hatches a plan to kill King Duncan. This shows that she is an ambitious woman …

Embedding quotations is another way of showing close attention to language

After Duncan's murder Lady Macbeth at first seems happy because all she ever wanted was to be Queen of Scotland. Macbeth cannot cope with what has happened. He was basically a good man but has committed evil and his mind begins to crumble. She now seems like the more ambitious one.

No evidence is given for this

Still clearly focused

A grade answer

Student B

Good use of accurate terminology

Shakespeare's *Macbeth* centres on the consequences of power and ambition. The protagonists Macbeth and Lady Macbeth embark on a journey to kill the present king in order to take the crown for themselves. This ambition is fuelled by the words of three witches who appear to Macbeth and his kinsman Banquo when on their way home from battle …

The theme is immediately addressed

This is the start of an introduction that shows secure understanding and gives an overview of events

Secure knowledge and reference to the text

Act 2 Scene 2 is particularly significant when charting the rise to power of the Macbeths. It is in this scene that Macbeth murders King Duncan. From this moment onwards there is no turning back and his ambition spirals out of control. Interestingly, it is in this scene where Lady Macbeth appears the stronger of the two. When he enters, clearly shaken by the enormity of his deed, she rebukes him: 'Infirm of purpose!' By insinuating that he is weak-minded, she is attempting to convince him that if they are to realise their ambitions, then he must pull himself together. Furthermore …

Confident use of a connective, showing engagement with the task

Good use of a short quotation, and exploration of the subtext

Now read the examiner's comments.

Examiner's comments

Student A has focused clearly on the theme and shows good understanding of the play. The response begins to discuss the characters with some insight, and to focus carefully on the language of the play. Relevant areas of the text are selected and highlighted, although points would need to be developed for this to reach a grade B. This is a grade C response.

Student B confidently focuses on the theme of the play, insightfully revealing that the *consequences* of power and ambition are key. The candidate successfully uses accurate technical vocabulary and explores the text in a perceptive way. Short quotations are selected and the subtext of the language is evaluated with secure understanding. The student is also able to link ideas together using sophisticated 'signpost' connectives such as 'interestingly' and 'furthermore'. This is a grade A response.

Activity

Use the grade checklists on pages 148–155 to suggest how Student A could improve her answer to gain a grade B and Student B could improve his answer to gain an A*.

Tackling the poems in relation to themes

The following section focuses on how to tackle the second bullet point of the question. This will always ask you to consider the poetry you have selected to write about. This is where you will need to discuss the poetry in relation to the theme of the question. Here you will be able to use the skills that you have developed in Section A of this book, when you focused on the poems individually. While you will want to focus on one poem in particular, it is important that you make reference to other poetry.

When you are working through your poems in Section A, it is useful to think of the following headings on the poetry pages as a way of progressing up the grade ladder:

- 'First thoughts': an initial understanding (grades G – F – E)
- 'Looking more closely': beginning to focus on language, structure, and form (grade D)
- 'Developing your ideas': building and linking detailed comments (grade C)
- 'Developing a personal response': close analysis (grades B – A – A*)

The following are key points to remember when studying your poems.

- Use a copy of the poem that you can annotate. As you read, underline key words and phrases, and make notes of your thoughts about them.
- Decide on an **overview** (your overall impression of the poem), then work out how your selected details fit into that overview.
- Start with the most obvious meanings in the poem, then work your way through to the **subtext** (reading between the lines).
- As well as commenting on the **content** (what the poem is about), comment on its **style** (how it is written).

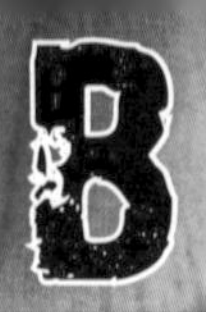

GradeStudio

Examiner tips

These are the areas that you should focus on in detail when studying a poem:

- **theme** (the ideas at the heart of the poem)
- **content** (what happens in the poem)
- **viewpoint** (the point of view or opinions of the speaker and/or poet)
- **mood** (the atmosphere/tone of the poem)
- **style** (techniques used by the poet and their effects).

Be careful not to merely 'spot features' by picking out techniques without analysing their effects. You don't get any extra marks for spotting how many similes are in the poem, for example. In fact, that type of approach can get in the way of showing your understanding.

A poem may have more than one theme. Do look for several themes in a poem; this will help you to develop a deeper understanding of the meanings.

Always bear in mind that the Shakespeare text will be linked by the same theme. Try to think of similarities and differences as you work through the poems and play. Jot down your ideas in the form of annotation on the text and notes in your exercise book/file.

Tackling the second bullet point

Now let us look at how you may approach tackling the poetry part of the controlled assessment. Consider the second part of the question on page 141:

Theme: Power and ambition

- Write about the way Shakespeare presents the theme of power and ambition. Focus initially on the events leading up to the death of King Duncan, and the relationship between Macbeth and Lady Macbeth shortly after the murder.
- Ted Hughes's poem 'Hawk Roosting' is also concerned with the theme of power and ambition. Write about the way the hawk is presented. In your answer you should also refer to other poetry that links to this theme.
- What is your personal response to the two pieces of literature? Try to make links between them.

This is the part of the question that we will focus on here – tackling the poem

Look at the following extracts from answers to the second bullet point of the question. One is a grade C response, and the other is a grade A response. Use the grade checklists on pages 148–155 to help you see the differences between the two grades.

C grade answer

Student A

The hawk describes himself as a killing machine: 'My manners are tearing off heads.' This makes him look powerful. He says 'There is no sophistry in my body'. 'Sophistry' means using an argument that seems clever, but is actually misleading.
This means that he thinks that he *is* clever and that there is nothing untrue about what he is saying. This makes him look quite arrogant.
When he says 'The sun is behind me' and 'the earth's face upward for my inspection', this quotation makes him sound god-like. He seems very ambitious, and acts as if he has all the power in the world. This is backed up by the line 'My eye has permitted no change.' This makes it look like he thinks he is in control . . .

Selecting and highlighting key areas. This could go further – picking out key words

There is no need to explain the meaning of any unusual words. You should concentrate on analysing the effect of the language choices

Is there a better way of phrasing this?

Unnecessary word! It is only a quotation because the student is quoting it. Best to avoid using this word in essays

A grade answer

Student B

From the outset, the speaker in Ted Hughes's 'Hawk Roosting' can be seen as a powerful creature. We are given an insight into the hawk's perspective on the world, as the poem is written in first-person narrative. This allows us to see how arrogant and self-assured he is. The fact that he sits 'in the top of the wood' can be taken two ways. Literally, he is positioned at the top of the wood, but also metaphorically he is at the top of the tree – at the top of the food chain. This is reinforced by the line 'I kill where I please because it is all mine.' The hawk's belief in his own power is clear here …
The power and ambition of the hawk can also be seen in the lines:
'Now I hold Creation in my foot.
Or fly up, and revolve it all slowly'
Here, he is suggesting that the world is only spinning because the hawk's claw turns it …

Probing subtext, looking for alternative meanings

Confident discussion of form and structure

Adding strength to the argument by finding extra evidence to support points made

Now read the examiner's comments.

Examiner's comments

Student A focuses well on the theme of the poem, but this answer is a little more mechanical. Explaining the definition of a word suggests that the candidate is not confident with the language. However, this response does go on to analyse the effect of the word 'sophistry'. Another indication that this is a more mechanical response is the use of the awkward phrase 'this quotation shows'. Overall, however, the response does show some insight and begins to explore the subtext. This is a grade C response.

Student B is confident, and immediately focuses on exploring the form of the poem. The candidate also explores the subtext carefully. Offering alternative meanings for specific words or phrases shows insight, and sometimes originality. Finding more than one thing to say about a selected quotation is also a sign of a confident and thoughtful writer. This is a grade A response.

Please note: As these are only extracts from complete answers, they do not contain references to other poems. Full answers would, however, need to contain such references.

Activity

Use the grade checklists on pages 148–155 to suggest how Student A could improve his answer to gain a grade B and Student B could improve her answer to gain a grade A*.

Tackling the third bullet point

This section focuses on how you can draw links and comparisons between texts. This will help you tackle the third bullet point of the question: This is the part of the question that we will focus on here – your personal response.

This part of the task will always ask you for your personal response to the texts, and invite you to discuss any links or comparisons that you have discovered in relation to the theme.

Theme: Power and ambition

- Write about the way Shakespeare presents the theme of power and ambition. Focus initially on the events leading up to the death of King Duncan, and the relationship between Macbeth and Lady Macbeth shortly after the murder.
- Ted Hughes's poem 'Hawk Roosting' is also concerned with the theme of power and ambition. Write about the way the hawk is presented. In your answer you should also refer to other poetry that links to this theme.
- What is your personal response to the pieces of literature? Try to make links between them.

This is the part of the question that we will focus on here – your personal response

How to write a successful comparative essay

Be clear about the links you want to make between the texts. Bear in mind that you need to link them by theme.

You may find it useful to make a list of similarities and differences between the texts in order to organise your ideas logically. For example, you may wish to draw up a table like the following.

Link	Macbeth	'Hawk Roosting'
Theme – ambition and power	Both Macbeth and Lady Macbeth are ambitious and want to become king and queen	The hawk is a powerful creature that seems ambitious to control the world
Form	Dialogue between characters allows us to see the extent of their ambitions	First-person narrative allows us to see the hawk's innermost feelings

Once you have made a list of what you want to discuss, organise your points logically so that each point will develop smoothly from one to another in your essay.

Try not to concentrate only on how the texts may be similar. You should also look for how they differ.

A *basic* comparative technique is as follows:

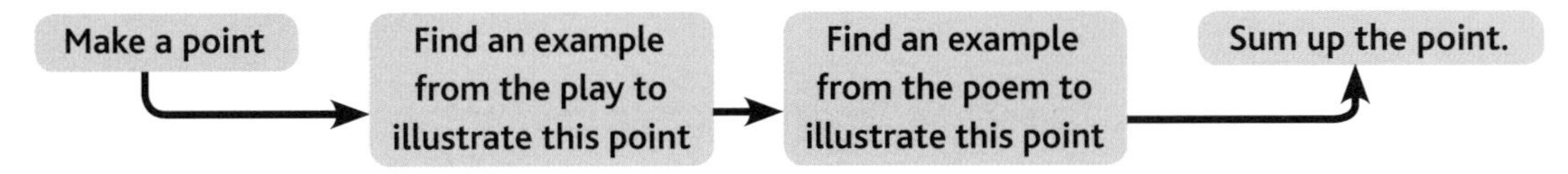

This is a very simple framework, and as you become more used to drawing links between texts you will not need it. More confident responses may move from text to text in a less systematic way. As long as you are making connections between the texts in relation to your theme, then you will be focusing correctly.

Hints and tips for essay writing

1 Keep your introduction short and simple.

2 Every time you want to use the text to support your ideas, follow these three steps:

- make your point
- back it up with a quotation
- explain how the quotation backs up your point.

This technique is often given a name such as the following:

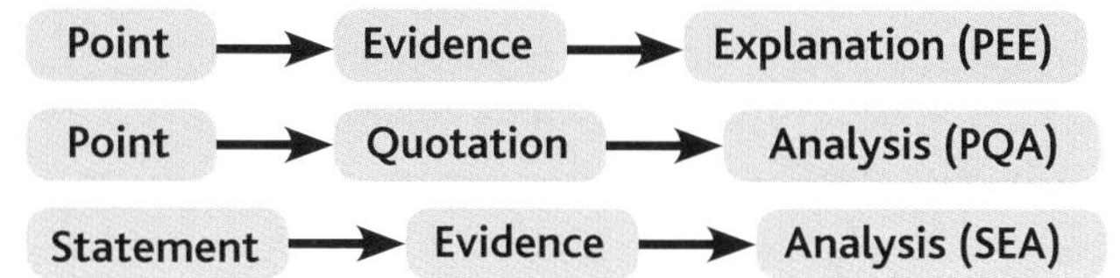

Using this technique focuses your response, gives you something relevant to discuss, and naturally leads to other points.

3 Write a brief conclusion to pull all your ideas together and neatly round off your essay.

Ways to introduce quotations

Think carefully about the best way to introduce your quotations. Shorter ones should be embedded within your own sentences. The following phrases will help:

implied by | reflected in | evident in | implicit in | evoked by | suggested by
shown by | portrayed in | apparent in | indicated by | conveyed by | revealed by

Activity

Try to think of how many other ways you could introduce your quotations.

Useful ways to compare/contrast

The following words and phrases can help you to structure sentences where you draw a comparison or a contrast.

equally	similarly	in the same way	as with	likewise
however	although	nevertheless	in contrast	on the other hand
accordingly	whereas	correspondingly	in comparison	comparably

Useful connectives

Aim to use connectives to 'signpost' the direction your essay is taking and to help you move smoothly from one point to the next. The following words and phrases can be useful.

because	as	alternatively	since	thus
significantly	therefore	moreover	furthermore	it would seem
it appears	it can be seen	additionally	although	despite

GradeStudio

Sample answers

Look at the following question and read the sample answers in the pages that follow, which answer the third bullet point. Can you identify how each student could progress up the grade ladder?

Theme: Power and ambition

- Write about the way Shakespeare presents the theme of power and ambition. Focus initially on the events leading up to the death of King Duncan, and the relationship between Macbeth and Lady Macbeth shortly after the murder.
- Ted Hughes's poem 'Hawk Roosting' is also concerned with the theme of power and ambition. Write about the way the hawk is presented. In your answer you should also refer to other poetry that links to this theme.
- What is your personal response to the pieces of literature? Try to make links between them.

G grade answer

In Shakespeare's play a man called Macbeth kills the king to get his power. Ted Hughes's poem 'Hawk Roosting' is about a hawk who thinks he is powerful. This is how the play and poem are linked.

Addresses theme in the play.

Addresses theme in the poem.

Makes a simple link between the two.

Now have a look at the grade criteria for a grade G. Does the student meet all of the criteria? Copy and complete the table below with your findings.

A student working at grade G will:	Yes	No	Not sure
✓ show familiarity with part(s) of the texts			
✓ make very simple comments about characters			
✓ make very simple comments about plot/content			
✓ make very simple comments about language			
✓ make very simple comments about meaning			
✓ make very simple links between the texts			
✓ make very simple comments on textual background* (* Only applies to English)			

Examiner's comments

This answer shows some familiarity with the theme. The student is able to make a very simple comment about the plot of *Macbeth* and the speaker in 'Hawk Roosting'.

How to improve this answer

The student needs to expand the discussion of characters and to refer to the text, perhaps using a quotation from a relevant area.

Now look at an extract from a grade F answer and the criteria for a grade F.

What are the main differences between a G and an F? Compare the two answers.
Has the student below met the F criteria? Copy and complete the table with your findings.

F grade answer

In *Macbeth* Shakespeare writes about Macbeth and Lady Macbeth who have a plan to kill the king and take over: 'Hail, King that shalt be!'
Ted Hughes writes about a hawk and how powerful he thinks he is: 'My manners are tearing off heads.' This makes them similar.

Selects relevant areas of the text, but ideas are not developed

General comment about how the characters are similar

A student working at grade F will:	Yes	No	Not sure
✓ make reference to part(s) of the texts			
✓ make general comments about characters			
✓ make general comments about plot/content			
✓ make general comments about language			
✓ make general comments about meaning			
✓ make some simple links between the texts			
✓ make simple comments on textual background*			

(* Only applies to English)

Examiner's comments

This answer does focus on the question, and is able to make simple links between Macbeth, Lady Macbeth and the hawk. The student makes a general comment about character and does make direct reference to the text, in the form of quotations. The quotations selected are relevant, but the student does nothing with them.

How to improve this answer

The student needs to develop the discussion of characters and to comment on the quotations selected, indicating why they are relevant.

Look at a piece of your own written work and consider whether you have fulfilled all the requirements for a grade F as shown in this checklist. If you answer 'No' or 'Not sure' to any of the items in the list, discuss them with your teacher and make a plan of how you will improve this aspect of your work.

Now look at this grade E answer and the examiner notes. Try to work out what makes it better than the grade F response. Use the grade E criteria box to help you.

What could this student do to progress up the grade ladder?

E grade answer

Shakespeare shows that Lady Macbeth wants to be a powerful character because she wants to kill the king so that Macbeth can become the new king: 'you shall put this night's great business into my dispatch'.

Ted Hughes also writes about power, but from the point of view of a hawk. We know that the hawk has a high opinion of itself: 'I kill where I please because it is all mine.'

This connecting word immediately shows that the student is making links

The selected quotations have not been explored. More development is needed.

A student working at grade E will:	Yes	No	Not sure
✓ have some focus on the question			
✓ respond to characters/situations/ideas			
✓ select areas of the text to discuss			
✓ make some comments about language/structure/form			
✓ make some comments about meaning			
✓ make some straightforward links and connections between the texts			
✓ have some awareness of social, cultural and historical contexts* (* Only applies to English)			

Examiner's comments

This answer begins to respond to the characters and to consider the reasons why they behave as they do. The student has selected relevant areas of the text and has made straightforward links between the texts. This is a grade E response.

How to improve this answer

The student needs to discuss the quotations selected, and begin to discuss the language used in both texts.

The following candidate is working at grade D. Read the extract below, and the notes the examiner has made. See whether you can identify how this student could progress up the grade ladder.

D grade answer

The theme of power/ambition is explored in *Macbeth* and 'Hawk Roosting'. Shakespeare focuses on Lady Macbeth's relationship with Macbeth. When Lady Macbeth learns about the witches' prophecy that Macbeth will become king, she hatches a plan to make it happen.
Ted Hughes also writes about ambition because the hawk in the poem wants to be the best: 'Now I hold Creation in my foot.' A difference between them is that the hawk is very confident about his own power, but Macbeth is too loyal to the king to be able to reach his ambition:
'We will proceed no further in this business.
He hath honoured me of late,'
Lady Macbeth is more ambitious than her husband ...

A sound point has been made, and a relevant quotation selected, but the quotation has not been analysed

Again, a comment about the selected quotation would improve this

Now read the examiner's comments below. How would you improve the student's answer so that it could achieve a grade C?

Examiner's comments

There are positive qualities to this answer: the focus on the question is clear and some similarities and differences are discussed. The student has made valid points, supported by well-chosen references to the texts. However, the student has not made detailed references to the texts or begun to discuss the subtext. This is an example of grade D writing.

How to improve this answer

Analysing the selected textual details would have pushed this answer to a grade C. Focusing on specific words is the key to looking at the text in detail.

Look at a piece of your own written work and consider whether you have fulfilled all the requirements for a grade D as shown below. If you answer 'No' or 'Not sure' to any of the items, discuss them with your teacher and make a plan of how you will improve this aspect of your work.

A student working at grade D will:	Yes	No	Not sure
✓ focus on the question			
✓ discuss characters/themes/mood and atmosphere			
✓ discuss language/structure/form			
✓ use relevant areas of the texts to support ideas			
✓ have an awareness of **subtext** (reading between the lines)			
✓ discuss some obvious similarities and differences between the texts			
✓ have some awareness of how social, cultural and historical contexts are relevant to understanding the texts* (* Only applies to English)			

Look at how a student working at grade C started to answer this part of the question. Read the paragraph from the student's answer below, and the notes the examiner made. See whether you can identify how this student could progress up the grade ladder.

C grade answer

Ted Hughes's poem 'Hawk Roosting' shows the world as seen from a hawk's point of view. The hawk seems very determined and powerful. Shakespeare also presents the theme of power and determination, but the difference is that he presents us with a husband and wife who plot to murder the king and take his crown. The hawk also has thoughts of murder: 'in sleep rehearse perfect kills'. The word 'rehearse' suggests that the hawk enjoys killing, and practises to make himself perfect – even when asleep. This also suggests that he is proud of himself. Similarly, in *Macbeth* Lady Macbeth is proud of her ambitious nature: 'O never/ Shall sun that morrow see.' She has murderous thoughts and that she will kill the king that night.

Selects key words and comments on them

Makes a second point about the same quotation

Uses a connective

Again, the quotation is analysed and the student makes detailed reference to the text

Examiner's comments

This answer is beginning to look at the texts in more detail. The response shows close reference to relevant areas of the text. Some interesting points are made and backed up with well-chosen quotations. The student has then analysed the quotations with some insight. Interestingly, the student has chosen to make two points about one of the quotations. This is evidence of 'going further' – developing ideas and building and linking detailed comments. The student is beginning to explore comparisons. The use of connectives is a good indicator of comparative work. This is a grade C response.

How to improve this answer

The points the student makes need to be developed. Close focus on language choices and how the texts are written would be useful too.

Look at a piece of your own written work and consider whether you have fulfilled all the requirements for a grade C as shown below. If you answer 'No' or 'Not sure' to any of the items, discuss them with your teacher and make a plan of how you will improve this aspect of your work.

A student working at grade C will:	Yes	No	Not sure
✓ discuss characters/themes/mood and atmosphere with some insight			
✓ discuss language/structure/form with some insight			
✓ make detailed reference to the texts to support ideas			
✓ explain how effects are achieved			
✓ begin to discuss the subtext			
✓ begin to explore comparisons of theme, content, viewpoint, mood and style			
✓ have a secure understanding of how the social, cultural and historical contexts have been influential to the texts* (* Only applies to English)			

Here is an extract from a grade B student response. Consider whether it fulfils all the grade B criteria, using the checklist below.

B grade answer

Macbeth and 'Hawk Roosting' both seem to be about power and ambition. In 'Hawk Roosting' the speaker is a hawk who describes his view of the world: 'The earth's face upward for my inspection.' This image suggests how the hawk is very confident that the world is there to suit his needs. It is in the form of a statement, which adds to the feeling of the hawk's confidence.

Lady Macbeth is also very powerful at the beginning of the play. She wants Macbeth to entertain the guests while she prepares to kill King Duncan. When hatching the plan, she says to her husband, 'Leave all the rest to me'. This implies that she feels that she is more capable to commit the crime than Macbeth. The audience will see her as more ambitious at this point.

Words such as 'suggest' show that the student is exploring the subtext thoughtfully

Analyses the structure of the text confidently

Again, using words such as 'implies' shows that the subtext is being examined

This is quite an assertive comment. Would everyone in the audience feel the same?

A student working at grade B will:	Yes	No	Not sure
✓ discuss characters/themes/mood and atmosphere thoughtfully and thoroughly			
✓ discuss language/structure/form thoughtfully and thoroughly			
✓ make detailed reference to the texts to support ideas			
✓ consider writers' intentions and purposes			
✓ discuss the subtext insightfully			
✓ explore the relevance and impact of connections and comparisons between texts			
✓ have a clear grasp of the social, cultural and historical contexts and how the texts relate to your own and others' experiences* (* Only applies to English)			

Examiner's comments

This answer is beginning to discuss the subtext of the texts in more detail. The response shows detailed reference to relevant areas of the texts. The student has analysed the quotations with insight and has started to explore form as well as language. The student shows a secure understanding of the plot/characters, and explores the motives of the characters.

The student is beginning to explore comparisons. The use of connectives is a good indicator of comparative work. This is a grade B response.

How to improve this answer

The student makes a sweeping assertion that the audience will feel a certain way towards Lady Macbeth. More sophisticated responses are more tentative, and offer alternatives. For example, using words such as 'arguably', 'perhaps' and 'may' when discussing an audience's reaction demonstrates that the writer knows there are several ways of reading a text.

Look at the following extract from a student working at grade A. Use the criteria for a grade A in the table below to consider whether this student has met the required standards, and to highlight what makes this answer an A.

A grade answer

Although *Macbeth* and 'Hawk Roosting' differ in form, there are distinct links that can be drawn between them. They both concern power and ambition and how a character's persona is formed by their self-belief, and what they are prepared to do to achieve their aims. In both texts we are given an insight into the characters' innermost thoughts. In 'Hawk Roosting', because the poem is written in the first person, in the form of a dramatic monologue, we gain a great insight into the speaker's confidence. The hawk starkly portrays how he feels that the world is there for his 'convenience'. He arrogantly describes how the 'air's buoyancy' and 'sun's ray' are 'of advantage' to him …

Similarly, Lady Macbeth initially believes that the crown is her right, and shows her desire for achieving it: 'Take my milk for gall, you murd'ring ministers.' The fact that she is calling on spirits to give her the strength to act implies that she will stop at nothing to achieve her aim. An audience may view this as a shocking, evil and ruthlessly ambitious act.

Immediately addresses similarities and differences

Going further, exploring the theme in detail

Addressing the form of both texts with insight

Selecting and embedding key quotations

Showing awareness that audience members could react differently to Lady Macbeth's actions

A student working at grade A will:	Yes	No	Not sure
✓ have a detailed and competent knowledge and understanding of the texts			
✓ analyse the texts confidently			
✓ explore writers' ideas/purposes sensitively			
✓ evaluate writers' use of language, structure and form			
✓ demonstrate an overview of the texts			
✓ sustain a discussion of links and comparisons between texts, selecting well-chosen details for cross-reference			
✓ comment on the importance of social, cultural and historical contexts and relate the texts to your own and others' experiences; show awareness of literary tradition* (* Only applies to English)			

Now read what the examiner noted about this answer below and at the top of the next page.

Examiner's comments

From the start this answer acknowledges the fact that the texts are different in form, and that although there are similarities, there are distinct differences also. The writing is confident and focused and makes several astute observations in a short space. Each point is supported insightfully. Also the style of writing is appropriately tentative, using words such as 'may'.

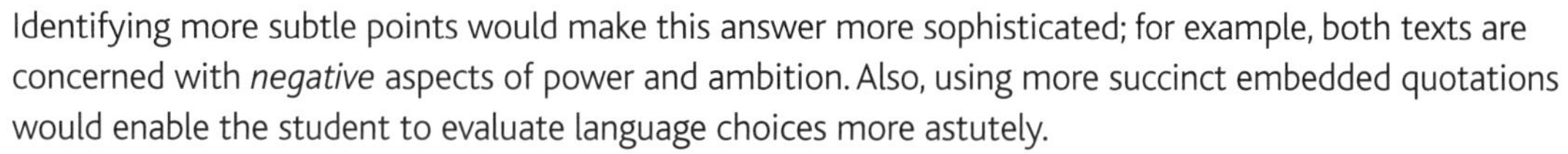

How to improve this answer
Identifying more subtle points would make this answer more sophisticated; for example, both texts are concerned with *negative* aspects of power and ambition. Also, using more succinct embedded quotations would enable the student to evaluate language choices more astutely.

Here is an extract from a student working at grade A*. Using the A* criteria, work out whether the student has met all of the requirements. Copy and complete the table below with your findings.

A* grade answer

Macbeth and 'Hawk Roosting' share some common ground in that they are concerned with the unpleasant side of power and ambition. The main characters in both texts appear to be overly confident and assured. 'Hawk Roosting' is a dramatic monologue spoken by a non-human voice; a hawk. We are provided with a series of images which depict the hawk's arrogance and pride. Indeed, the hawk is brimming with superiority: 'It took the whole of Creation / To produce my foot, my each feather.' The hawk is seemingly bragging and delighting in how magnificent it appears.

This can be directly compared to Lady Macbeth. The way she belittles her husband, referring to him as 'afeard' and 'a coward' reveals her merciless ambition to become queen. She, like the hawk, feels that she deserves to be 'great', and wants her husband to share the power; he calls her 'My dearest partner of greatness'...

A subtle point being made here – the 'unpleasant' nature of the theme is highlighted

Using words like 'seemingly' shows a confident understanding of alternative readings

The use of short, embedded quotations allows the student to examine the language confidently

Making confident links

A student working at grade A* will:	Yes	No	Not sure
✓ show a comprehensive and sophisticated knowledge and understanding of the texts			
✓ analyse the texts with confidence and succinctness			
✓ explore writers' ideas/purposes sensitively and critically			
✓ evaluate writers' use of language, structure and form and their effects on readers			
✓ demonstrate a developed and perceptive overview of the texts			
✓ make subtle points of comparison and probe links confidently			
✓ demonstrate a clear understanding of social, cultural and historical contexts and explain how texts have been/are influential at different times* (* Only applies to English)			

Examiner's comments

From the start this answer acknowledges the fact that the texts are different in form, and that although there are similarities, there are distinct differences also. The writing is confident and focused and makes several astute observations in a short space. Each point is supported insightfully. Also the style of writing is appropriately tentative, using words such as 'may'.

Heinemann is an imprint of Pearson Education Limited, a company incorporated in England and Wales, having its registered office at Edinburgh Gate, Harlow, Essex, CM20 2JE. Registered company number: 872828

www.pearsonschoolsandfecolleges.co.uk

Heinemann is a registered trademark of Pearson Education Limited

Text © Pearson Education Limited 2010

First published 2010

12 11 10
10 9 8 7 6 5 4 3 2 1

British Library Cataloguing in Publication Data
A catalogue record for this book is available from the British Library

ISBN 978 0 435014 35 3

Copyright notice
All rights reserved. No part of this publication may be reproduced in any form or by any means (including photocopying or storing it in any medium by electronic means and whether or not transiently or incidentally to some other use of this publication) without the written permission of the copyright owner, except in accordance with the provisions of the Copyright, Designs and Patents Act 1988 or under the terms of a licence issued by the Copyright Licensing Agency, Saffron House, 6–10 Kirby Street, London EC1N 8TS (www.cla.co.uk). Applications for the copyright owner's written permission should be addressed to the publisher.

Design and produced by Kamae Design, Oxford
Original illustrations © Pearson Education Limited 2010
Illustrated by Leo Brown (p46, 117), Rory Walker (p102)
Cover design by Wooden Ark Studios, Leeds
Picture research by Sally Cole
Cover photo/illustration © Corbis
Printed in the UK by Scotprint

Acknowledgements
The author and publisher would like to thank the following individuals and organisations for permission to reproduce photographs:
DAVID NOBLE PHOTOGRAPHY/Alamy and Kleve Photography/Alamy p2; Bertrand Gardel/Hemis/Corbis p4; Christie's Images/CORBIS p7; Larus Karl Ingason/Photolibrary pp8–9; The British Library/Photolibrary p10; Lebrecht Music and Arts Photo Library/Alamy p11; Keith Glover/Alamy p12; Zia Soleil/Getty Images pp14, 15; Science & Society Picture. Getty Images p17; Stephen Mallon/Getty Images pp18, 19; Ian Shaw/Getty Images p20; A. Inden/Corbis p22; SuperStock/Getty Images p24; Ilona Wellmann/Photolibrary p26; Symphonie/Getty Images p28; Peter Widmann/Photolibrary p31; Chad Ehlers/Photolibrary p32; Edwin H Remsberg/GettyImages pp34–35; ;Edward Parker/Alamy p37; Shutterstock p38; Hulton Archive/Getty Images p40; Gary D Landsman/Photolibrary p42; Stockbroker Stockbroker/Photolibrary p44; Fine Art Photographic Library/Photolibrary p49; Topical Press Agency/Stringer/Getty Images p50; Adam Burton/Alamy pp52–53; Ypps Ypps/Photolibrary p54; Gisela Delpho/Photolibrary pp56–57; Bronzino,Agnolo(1503-1572),school: portrait of Lucrezia di Cosimo 1.Florence,Galleria degli Uffizi© 1990.Photo Scala,Florence-courtesy of the Ministero Beni Att.Culturali p59; Bob Krist/Corbis p60; ERMAL ETA/Stringer/Getty Images p63; Sean Ellis/Getty Images p64; Jed Share/Getty Images p66; Juan Manuel Silva/Photolibrary p69; Anthony-Masterson/Getty Images p70; Maria Mosolova/Photolibrary p72; Young Woman with Letter and Locket, 1667 (oil on panel) by Netscher, Caspar (1639-84) p75; Philip Kramer/Getty Images pp76–77; Jose Luis Pelaez/Getty Images pp78–79; nagelestock.com/Alamy p80–81; The Print Collector/Alamy p83; David Tipling/Photolibrary p84; Backhuysen, Ludolf 1631-1708. "Storm at a mountainous coast", c.1675. Oil on canvas, 173.5 x 341cm. Brussels, Musees Royaux des Beaux-Arts / AKG p86; The Print Collector/Photolibrary p88; Jodi Cobb/Getty Images p90; Burstein Collection/CORBIS p93; Ray Wise/Getty Images p95; Robert Dowling/CORBIS p96; Cristian Baitg/Getty Images pp98–99; Photolibrary p100–101; Scott Thomas/Corbis p104; Bettmann/Corbis p106; C Lyttle/Photolibrary p108; SSPL via Getty Images p110–111; Associated Newspapers /Rex Features p113; Michael Breuer/Photolibrary p114–115; Hulton-Deutsch Collection/CORBIS p118; Topham / Fotomas p120; Colin Garratt; Milepost 92½/CORBIS p123; The Print Collector/Photolibrary p124; Mary Evans Picture Library p127; Steve Porter/Alamy p128; Douglas McCarthy/Mary Evans Picture Library p137; Robbie Jack/Corbis p139.

Every effort has been made to contact copyright holders of material reproduced in this book. Any omissions will be rectified in subsequent printings if notice is given to the publishers.

'Valentine' taken from *Mean Time* by Carol Ann Duffy © Carol Ann Duffy. Published by Anvil Press Poetry in 1993. Used by permission; 'A Frosty Night' from *Complete Poems in One Volume* by Robert Graves, © 1993. Used by permission of Carcanet Press and AP Watt Ltd; 'Long Distance II' by Tony Harrison is used by kind permission of Tony Harrison. *Tony Harrison Selected Poems* (Penguin 1987) & *Collected Poems* (Penguin 2007); 'Catrin' by Gillian Clarke, from *Gillian Clarke Collected Poems*, © 1997. Published by Carcanet Press. Used by permission; 'Follower' by Seamus Heaney from *Open Ground: Poems 1966–1996.* Used by permission of Faber and Faber Ltd; 'What Has Happened to Lulu' by Charles Causley from *Collected Poems for Children* published by Macmillan. Used by kind permission of David Higham Associates; 'Mid-Term Break' by Seamus Heaney from *Open Ground: Poems 1966–1996.* Used by permission of Faber and Faber Ltd; 'The Almond Tree' From *Rounding the Horn: Collected Poems* by Jon Stallworthy © 1998. Published by Carcanet Press. Used with permission; 'Prayer Before Birth' from *Collected Poems* by Louis MacNeice, © Louis MacNeice, 1966. Published by Faber & Faber. Used by permission of David Higham Associates; 'My Grandmother' from *New Collected Poems* by Elizabeth Jennings published by Carcanet. Used by permission of David Higham Associates; 'Old Age Gets Up' by Ted Hughes from *Collected Poems.* Used by permission of Faber and Faber Ltd; 'Sweet 18' from *Selected Poems* by Sheenagh Pugh. Copyright © 1990. Published by Seren Books. Used by permission of Seren Books; 'Do Not Go Gentle Into That Good Night' from the *Poems* by Dylan Thomas. Used by permission of David Higham Associates; 'I Have Longed to Move Away' from *Poems* by Dylan Thomas. Used by permission of David Higham Associates; extract from *The Collected Letters of Dylan Thomas* used by permission of David Higham Associates; 'Leisure' by H M Davies is used by permission of Kieron Griffin as Trustee of the Mrs H M Davies Will Trust; 'Human Interest' by Carol Ann Duffy © Carol Ann Duffy taken from *Standing Female Nude.* Published by Anvil Press Poetry in 1985. Used by permission; 'Hawk Roosting' by Ted Hughes from *Collected Poems.* Used by permission of Faber and Faber Ltd; 'The Interrogation' by Edwin Muir from *Collected Poems.* Used by permission of Faber And Faber Ltd; 'They Did Not Expect This' by Vernon Scannell. Used by kind permission of The Estate of Vernon Scannell; 'Meeting Point' from *Collected Poems* by Louis MacNeice, © Louis MacNeice, 1966. Published by Faber & Faber. Used by permission of David Higham Associates; 'Afternoons' by Philip Larkin from *Collected Poems.* Used by permission of Faber and Faber Ltd; 'Havisham' taken from *Mean Time* by Carol Ann Duffy © Carol Ann Duffy. Published by Anvil Press Poetry in 1993. Used by permission; 'Twice Shy' by Seamus Heaney from *Open Ground; Poems 1966–1996.* Used by permission of Faber and Faber Ltd; 'Song of the Worker's Wife' by Alice Gray Jones, translated by Katie Gramich; 'A Married State' by Katherine Philips. Used by permission of Hono Press; 'Chapel Deacon' by R.S. Thomas. From *Collected Poems 1945–1990* published by JM Dent. Used by kind permission of JM Dent, an imprint of The Orion Publishing Group, Ltd; 'The Hunchback in the Park' from *Poems* by Dylan Thomas. Used by permission of David Higham Associates; 'Displaced Person Looks at a Caged Bird' from *Some Men are Brothers* by D.J. Enright © 1960. Used by kind permission of Watson, Little Ltd; 'Base Details' from *War Poems* by Siegfried Sassoon. Copyright © Siegfried Sassoon by kind permission of the Estate of George Sassoon; 'The Capon Clerk' from *Selected Poems* by Sheenagh Pugh. Copyright © 1990. Published by Seren Books. Used by permission of Seren Books; 'You will be hearing from us shortly' by U.A. Fanthorpe, from *Collected Poems 1978–2003.* Published by Peterloo Poets. Used by permission; 'Refugee Blues (Say This City)' by W.H. Auden from *Collected Poems.* Used by permission of Faber and Faber Ltd; 'A Refusal to Mourn the Death, by Fire, of a Child in London' from *Poems* by Dylan Thomas. Used by permission of David Higham Associates; 'The Conscript', taken from *Poems 1904–1917* by WW Gibson © 1923. Published by Macmillan. Used by permission of Macmillan and the Trustees of the Estate of W.W. Gibson; 'MCMXIV' by Philip Larkin from *Collected Poems.* Used by permission of Faber and Faber Ltd; 'The Hero' from *War Poems* by Siegfried Sassoon. Copyright © Siegfried Sassoon by kind permission of the Estate of George Sassoon.